FORAGING THE OZARKS

HELP US KEEP THIS GUIDE UP TO DATE

Every effort has been made by the author and editors to make this guide as accurate and useful as possible. However, many things can change after a guide is published—regulations change, techniques evolve, facilities come under new management, etc.

We appreciate hearing from you concerning your experiences with this guide and how you feel it could be improved and kept up to date. While we may not be able to respond to all comments and suggestions, we'll take them to heart and we'll also make certain to share them with the author. Please send your comments and suggestions to the following address:

FalconGuides
Reader Response/Editorial Department
246 Goose Lane, Suite 200
Guilford, CT 06437

Thanks for your input!

FORAGING THE OZARKS

Finding, Identifying, and Preparing
Edible Wild Foods in the Ozarks

Bo Brown

Happy Foraging, enjoy!

Bo Brown

FALCONGUIDES

GUILFORD, CONNECTICUT

FALCONGUIDES®

An imprint of The Rowman & Littlefield Publishing Group, Inc.
4501 Forbes Blvd., Ste. 200
Lanham, MD 20706
www.rowman.com

Falcon and FalconGuides are registered trademarks and Make Adventure Your Story is a trademark of The Rowman & Littlefield Publishing Group, Inc.

Distributed by NATIONAL BOOK NETWORK

Photos by Bo Brown unless otherwise noted
Map by The Rowman & Littlefield Publishing Group, Inc.

British Library Cataloguing-in-Publication Information available

Library of Congress Control Number: 2020933529

ISBN 978-1-4930-4257-9 (paper : alk. paper)
ISBN 978-1-4930-4258-6 (electronic)

Printed in Malaysia

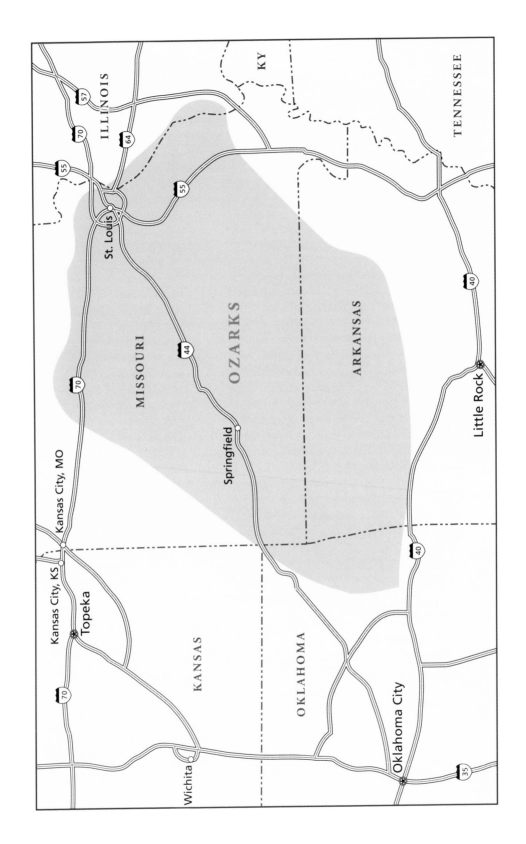

CONTENTS

ACKNOWLEDGMENTS

My mother, **Parthenia Jane Brown,** grew up in dirt-poor Depression-era rural Arkansas. Her family rode out those hard times on a subsistence farm and, like many in that situation, had to occasionally depend on foraging to survive. She instilled my lifelong love of the outdoors during our countless fishing and foraging trips, and taught me about hunting, wild plants, and nature in general. I'm grateful that at an early age, she allowed me the indulgence of unsupervised all-day meanders to fish, hunt, and explore the nearby creeks and woods.

Chief Jim "Fire Eagle" Boose and former bandmate and backpacking buddy **Don Brink** were instrumental in guiding me to a life of teaching primitive skills and foraging. During the summer of 1977, I was working as a musician at the Branson, Missouri, theme park "Silver Dollar City," where Fire Eagle was demonstrating flint knapping and plant lore. Don and I had already been foraging a bit on our frequent outings, and the two of us began to spend our free time at Fire Eagle's display, mesmerized by his knowledge and stories.

Those experiences lit the fire, and our discovery of wilderness survival books by Larry Dean Olsen and Tom Brown Jr. turned our backpack trips into bushcraft practice sessions and eventual careers in teaching outdoor skills. Don also introduced me to birding, prompted by his friend and avid birder, Dick Addison. I got the birding "bug" and literally fell into a life of traveling the country to work on songbird studies. Fire Eagle often said, "All knowledge is incomplete till it's passed on," and Don's friend Dick always said, "Teaching is just planting seeds." Those seemed like good rules to live by.

Dr. Kim Smith and **Dr. Jane Fitzgerald**—Thanks for hiring this unschooled and unqualified, but highly enthusiastic, nature geek in 1985 for my first songbird research job, an adventure that continues today. That work provided an opportunity to learn volumes from people who knew far more than I ever would about the natural sciences.

Emily Higgins—Providence is when you begin a big writing project and learn that your singer-songwriter bandmate is a professional proofreader for the local public school system. Thanks for the invaluable proofing skills and beautiful music.

Dr. Kitty Ledbetter provided expertise and critical guidance of the process in its initial stages. I may have not landed this one without her help.

Marideth Sisco—In our thirty-five years of friendship and music, she always prodded me to write a book, and it finally happened! Thanks for the advice, technical help, and for the belief that I had something worthwhile to contribute.

Denise Thomas—A special thanks to my love and partner for the last-minute editing assistance, her steadfast encouragement and patience during this endeavor, and for always knowing when to tell me to go to the woods.

Much of our early understanding of North American plant uses were from contacts with indigenous tribes, who nurtured an intimate relationship with the flora and fauna of their natural world; we owe them much gratitude for maintaining and passing along that body of knowledge.

Several authors were influential in my early education in plants. My dog-eared copies of foraging books by Euell Gibbons, Bradford Angier, the Foxfire Book series, Tom Brown Jr., Arkansas's own Billy Jo Tatum, and regional Ozarks wildflower identification guides by Edgar Denison and Don Kurz provided a wealth of fodder for my obsession. Samuel Thayer, Christopher Nyerges, Green Deane, Pascal Baudar, and others continue to push the boundaries and provide inspiration; and folks like our local foraging educator Rachel Elizabeth (*Once Upon a Weed*) and permaculture homesteader/writer Wren Haffner (*Ozark Mountain Jewel*) give me hope that young people will continue to do so.

And finally, thanks to all my talented and supportive friends in the communities of music, natural sciences, and primitive skills. I'm blessed to be surrounded by such inspirational and talented characters, even those who point at me in a crowded room and shout, "Hey, that guy eats weeds and bugs!" (You know who you are.)

INTRODUCTION

Over the years, I've had several conversations about foraging that started with some form of this question: "Why would I want to go out and spend time learning about and looking for wild plants when I can go to the supermarket and buy great food?" Entire books are devoted to this question. My foraging journey started in childhood, but it didn't expand much till I got interested in wilderness survival. The goal of "living off the land" on backpack trips developed into the desire to teach about nature and the old ways, and as of late, the journey has taken more of a culinary focus. My question now is, "Why wouldn't you want to learn about foraging?" Those who take the time will find a sense of connection when making food from wild-gathered sources. Foraging binds us to our ancestral past of living with and from nature, getting us out of our boxes and into new places where we often meet other people on the same learning path.

The numerous "reality" TV shows featuring wilderness survival and disaster prepping, foraging groups on social media, and a series of new print publications have vaulted foraging into nearly mainstream status. Wild foods are also appearing in the creations of high-cuisine chefs, "Farm to Table" dinners, and in the "Slow Food" and "Re-Wilding" movements. Many people seek to know more about the provenance of the foods they eat and are seeking new culinary experiences in the process. Foraging is the ultimate way to realize those goals.

It is increasingly important in this age of industrially-produced foods to know the source and growing conditions of our food supply. (See appendix D, Industrial Food vs. Wild Food.) The rising number of food recalls, foodstuffs grown in other countries under questionable conditions, and research showing detectable levels of agricultural chemicals in human breast milk and body tissue should make us think more about what we put into our bodies.

From a health standpoint, decades of studies show that wild plants are consistently more nutrient-dense and vitamin-rich than domesticated plants. They also contain more medicinal compounds, such as anthocyanins, polyphenols, and other phytonutrients, while offering a wide range of flavors not found in supermarkets. Simply adding foraged foods to your existing diet can help make up for the nutritional and medicinal shortcomings in our commercial food supply. It also provides another reason to explore the outdoors in our beautiful Ozarks!

Scope of This Book

This work is intended to be an easy-to-use field reference for both beginning and seasoned foragers to aid in finding, identifying, and preparing the Ozarks' wealth of wild edibles. It features detailed descriptions written in field-guide style, and features color photos of common native and nonnative plants. It also includes several species that may have been overlooked in other references. A few botanical terms were used for brevity's sake, and a glossary of terms is included. Most plant species were selected for their ability to provide food throughout the different seasons; others were chosen for their interesting flavors in culinary and beverage use. Recipes and processing tips are included to aid in preparing your harvested bounty. Most entries only mention general medicinal use, to encourage further study for those so inclined. Specific medicinal and utilitarian uses were included, when prominent. Toxic lookalikes or cautions are included in the "Warnings/Comments" sections. Mushrooms were excluded, as they are covered well in the Missouri Department of Conservation's recent book, *Missouri's Wild Mushrooms*, and other publications dedicated to mycology. A brief segment on edible insects is provided in appendix C. If you have ideas for plants, plant uses, or recipes that weren't covered here, please contact the author at firstearth.org to include them in future revisions.

Organization

This book is organized in the system used by botanists. Plants are grouped into general classes (clades) of Magnoliids, Eudicots, and Monocots and are listed by their Latin family names in alphabetical order. Common names, genus, and species are included, and a reference list of plants by food type and season can be found in appendix B. A general understanding of plant families will aid in identifying characteristics common to each. This knowledge will help in recognizing new plants when found out of context, and will hopefully lead to more study and better overall identification skills.

General Foraging Guidelines / Ethical and Safe Collection

The popularity and recent media attention given to foraging has provided possibilities for negative environmental impacts, especially when the ethics, safety, and legality of collecting plants are overlooked. Considering human overpopulation and the finite amount of wildlands available, it isn't feasible for the entire population to adopt foraging as a sole means of feeding themselves. However, most habitats can produce plenty of wild food for harvest without significant effect, especially when foragers are educated in best practices and are aware of their impacts. And luckily, many edible plants are found in non-pristine habitats and are considered to be pests or weeds. These and others will grow under less-than-optimal conditions and can be propagated from seed and grown in low-maintenance "weed gardens" where feasible. When people are informed about the possibilities, native/edible landscaping can be done in urban/suburban conditions, and in habitats recovering from environmental damage. This will promote more effective native food production for both humans and wildlife.

Cincinnati, Ohio–based Indigenous Landscapes and other companies and organizations are making great strides in their work to reestablish beneficial native plant communities, working in both practice and education.

Never consume wild plants unless you are 100 percent sure of identification! Please take the time to cross-reference your ID with several sources, and never depend on plant identification phone apps or foraging/edible plant groups on social media. I've witnessed multiple instances of dangerous plants misidentified as edible on those sources.

Introduced vs. Native—The plant names are listed with "native" or "introduced" in the header to provide an indication as to how much, or whether, to harvest. Many common introduced plants are widespread and found in a number of habitats, so they can be collected in large volume without consequence. The "invasivore" movement is now trending in many areas, where foragers focus on collecting only invasive plants or animals for food as a way to mitigate the environmental and economic damage they may cause. Native plants are often more restricted in range and to specific habitats, so only collect them where found in abundance, and always protect the plant's ability to reproduce. If you encounter just a few individuals of a desired plant while collecting, sample a few leaves and move on to something more abundant. An effective way to increase the population of less-common desirable native plants is to gather seeds for planting or use those left over from processing to plant in other suitable habitats. Several invasive and environmentally damaging species are listed in this book; always take care to avoid distributing the seeds of those plants into new areas.

Digging roots—Root collection is prohibited on public land. If you don't have access to foraging areas, private landowners and farmers will often allow it with permission; always ask first. When digging roots, spread your activities over a large area, and when collecting from colonies, take a few here and a few there. A good rule is to never take more than 30 percent of the plants that are present; a bit of thinning can actually improve the vigor and life of a colony over time. Overharvest by commercial root diggers and unscrupulous market wildcrafters has negatively impacted populations of several valuable native species in some areas. Ginseng (*Panax americana*), goldenseal (*Hydrastis canadensis*), ramps (*Allium tricoccum*), coneflower species in the genus *Echinacea*, and a few others have suffered regional population declines due to their popularity and marketability. Always be aware of your impacts, and make them positive whenever possible.

Legality—All public lands, public roadsides, and public waterways have regulations for collecting plants, and the rules are varied: Federal and state lands prohibit digging roots, but many allow collection of greens, fruits, berries, nuts, and mushrooms for personal consumption. Some public parks may ban all collection except what is eaten within the park, and some areas allow collection only with a collection permit, issued at the supervisor's discretion. Be sure to always check first before collecting, as fines for prohibited activities can be quite steep.

Allergic reactions to certain plants—These reactions seem to be on the increase, many from exposure to common foods like peanuts and wheat. When consuming a new plant for the first time, try only a small sample and wait for a while to make sure there isn't an unpleasant reaction.

Pollution—When collecting from ditches, roadsides, edges of pastures, or agricultural fields, be aware that these areas may be susceptible to pollution by herbicide/pesticide spraying or agricultural runoff.

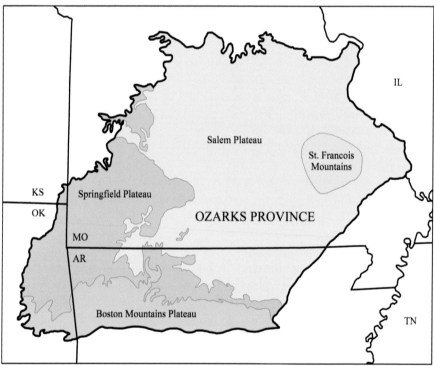

IMAGE BY DUSTIN THOMPSON

THE OZARKS PHYSIOGRAPHIC REGION

The Ozarks comprise the most extensive highland region between the Appalachians and the Rockies, encompassing the southern half of Missouri, northwest Arkansas, and small segments of southwestern Illinois, southeastern Kansas, and northeastern Oklahoma. When included with the Ouachita Mountains in west-central Arkansas and adjoining northeastern Oklahoma, the entire region is known as the US Interior Highlands. Precambrian volcanic activity in what is now southeastern Missouri formed a broad dome of granite and rhyolite, forming the St. Francois Mountains. Areas to the west and south are characterized by a series of uplifted sedimentary plateaus that are deeply dissected by a billion years of erosion. The Salem and Springfield Plateaus are underlain with Ordovician and Mississippian dolostones and limestones, respectively, which are interspersed with chert layers. The Boston Mountains at the southern edge of the uplift are capped by Pennsylvanian sandstone and shale. The underlying porous layers of limestone in the region creates karst topography, leading to the formation of numerous caves, sinkholes, springs, fens, and crystal-clear spring-fed rivers; Big Spring in the Current River Valley is one of the largest springs in the world.

Much of the Ozarks' rugged terrain is covered in diverse forest habitat dominated by oak and hickory, with scattered stands of shortleaf pine. Numerous bald knobs and open glades occur in the uplands, where bedrock near or at the surface prohibits deep root systems for most trees. Eastern red cedar has a shallower root system and can dominate glade habitats if not managed. These rocky openings—islands of near-desert and prairie habitat surrounded by forest—contain a distinctly unique plant community. Glades also host fauna usually found further south and west, such as the greater roadrunner, eastern collared lizard, brown tarantula, striped scorpion, and the 8-inch-long and venomous giant red-headed centipede. The cool, wet habitats of springs, fens, and cave entrances can harbor "glacial relict" plants, holdovers from when the northern half of Missouri was glaciated. The Ozarks' deep forest cover, plateau-prairies, clearings for agriculture, and other natural physiological features provide conditions for a high degree of biological diversity—and a wealth of foraging opportunities.

POISONOUS PLANTS

Below is a list of plants that contain dangerous to potentially fatal levels of toxins if ingested. Poison ivy and its relatives contain oils that can cause a severe dermatitis rash. There are many other toxic plants present, but these are the most dangerous if consumed by mistake. Several plants listed in this book have edible fruits when ripe, but unripe fruits and other parts may be toxic. Mayapple, ground plum, ground cherry, pawpaw, and elderberry fall into this category. Some plants need to be boiled to cook off the toxins, as with pokeweed.

EASTERN DEATH CAMAS
Toxicoscordian nutallii

Native

Family: Melanthiaceae
This showy perennial emerges from a bulb as a basal rosette of 6–10 erect, linear leaves, surrounded by a papery sheath at the base. As the central flowering stem emerges, the leaves grow up to 15" long and ¾" wide, becoming thick, stout, and arching. The smooth stem forms as a raceme with cream-white flowers about ½" across. It is similar in structure and appearance to the edible *Camassia scilloides* (wild hyacinth), but is generally stouter in appearance, and its flower petals are white, shorter, broader, and on longer stalks compared to *C. scilloides*. The bulbs of the two plants may be difficult to differentiate, so if collecting wild hyacinth, identify the plants while flowering to make sure the entire colony is the same species and doesn't have death camas growing within it. *Anticlea elegans* (mountain death camas) is a slightly more common toxic relative. Both are listed as present but rare in parts of the Ozarks, but I've never encountered them. These plants contain the neurotoxic alkaloids zygacine and zygadenine and, given their acute toxicity, are good to be aware of and to avoid.

FALSE HELLEBORE (AKA WOOD'S BUNCHFLOWER, VIRGINIA BUNCHFLOWER)
Melanthium woodii, M. virginicum

Native

Family: Melanthiaceae

This uncommon, showy perennial is conspicuous in the spring for its large basal rosette of pleated leaves. Individual leaves emerge from a bulb, are elliptical to ovate, up to 1' long, with prominent lateral veins and smooth margins. Plants are usually found in close proximity on lower portions of north-facing slopes and bluffs, in moist forests in the eastern two-thirds of the Ozarks. The flowering stem is usually 2'–4' tall, branched, and bearing small flowers. *M. virginicum* has white flowers; *M. woodii* has purple to reddish-brown flowers. Both species are extremely toxic and can cause rapid cardiac arrest. Several reports exist of hikers being poisoned by mistaking basal leaves and root bulbs of false hellebore for *Allium tricoccum* (ramps, wild leeks), a wild onion species that is popular with foragers. Ramps are quite rare in most of the Ozarks and are declining across parts of their range due to overharvest and are not included in this book.

POISON HEMLOCK
Conium maculatum

Introduced

Family: Apiaceae

Poison hemlock is a vigorous and aggressive biennial that emerges from a taproot as a basal rosette. Basal leaves are up to 12" long and across, generally triangular in shape. Leaflets are double or triple bipinnately compound, with a lacy appearance. The second-year flowering stem is up to 8' tall, with longitudinal veins that give it a ribbed appearance. The stem is smooth and hollow, with purple spots on the lower half and a whitish bloom on the surface that easily wipes off; it develops alternate leaves that become smaller as they ascend the stem. Small, white flowers emerge in midsummer, forming on loosely-clustered, rounded umbels at the stem and branch terminus. The large, mature taproot has a generally disagreeable smell and contains hollow chambers. Emerging young basal leaves of poison hemlock appear generally thicker and more robust when compared with the sparser and generally hairy foliage of *D. carota* (wild carrot). Carrot roots will always have the characteristic carrot odor. All parts of the plant contain the toxin coniine, which has a chemical structure similar to nicotine, but the taproot contains the highest concentration. This toxin disrupts the central nervous system, and even a small dose can cause respiratory collapse and death.

Poison hemlock basal leaves

WATER HEMLOCK (AKA SPOTTED COWBANE)
Cicuta maculata

Native

Family: Apiaceae

Water hemlock's flower structure and general plant structure is similar to poison hemlock. Its hollow, flowering stems are up to 6' tall, smooth, green to purplish, often with longitudinal veins. Compound leaves are up to 1' long, odd-pinnate or doubly odd-pinnate; leaflets are up to 4" long and 1¼" wide, linear or lanceolate to ovate-elliptic, often with coarsely toothed margins. Like poison hemlock, its mature taproot contains hollow chambers. All parts of the plant contain cicutoxin, a highly poisonous unsaturated alcohol with a strong odor. The toxin is found principally in the taproot but is also present in the leaves and stems during early growth. This plant is responsible for the highest number of deaths from being mistakenly identified as similar edible species, such as wild parsnip. Many sources suggest avoidance of all plants in the family Apiaceae with a similar appearance until their physical characteristics are fully understood and positive identification is absolute.

POISON IVY, POISON OAK
Toxicodendron radicans, T. pubescens

Native

Family: Anacardiaceae

Poison ivy is common, even rampant, in many parts of the Ozarks. An extremely variable plant, it can appear as a ground cover, a small to large woody vine over 4" in diameter and climbing trees up to 60', or grow as a low upright shrub to 5'. The saying "Leaves of three, let it be" isn't always helpful, as many nontoxic and edible plants also have three leaflets.

Poison ivy has alternate, trifoliate leaves on long, slender petioles, and the center leaflet is on a much longer stalk than the two laterals. The blade surface can be dull or shiny, with margins that are entire, lobed, or broadly and sparsely toothed. The vines are attached to trees or other substrates by aerial rootlets. Sparse panicles of small, yellowish-white flowers form across from the leaf axils. Flowers mature to green and eventually white, round drupes about ¼" across. *T. pubescens* (poison oak) is similar, but has rounded leaflets, grows as an upright shrub rather than a climbing vine, and has a more southern range.

Not everyone is affected by the urushiol oils, and some that have never had a reaction may become allergic at some point. For those who are allergic, the best preventative measure is to scrub all parts of the skin that may have been exposed with soap and cold water, even areas that may have not been initially exposed. The oil is persistent and can remain on dead vines, clothing, gloves, and tools for quite a long time. When contacted, it can spread easily to other parts of the body; it can be transferred to your skin from your clothing when removing them, or even by petting your dog or cat after it has been exposed. After the rash develops, there are several over-the-counter and prescription medicines available. Effective plant medicines for the rash are jewelweed (*Impatiens* spp.) and broad-leaved plantain (*Plantago* spp.). The fresh leaves and stems are crushed or put in a blender to bring up the sap and are applied to the affected area as a poultice, which is changed twice daily until the rash subsides. According to those who use it, the poultice will dry and heal the rash several days before untreated areas heal. The leaves don't keep long after harvest, but they can be processed in a blender with a bit of water and frozen in ice-cube trays, or the leaves can be put in a jar and covered with alcohol to make a tincture.

MAGNOLIIDS

This group (clade) was formerly classed within the eudicots and is part of a larger group of primitive flowering plants called basal angiosperms. Its members may exhibit characteristics of both eudicots and monocots. Together, they are the three main divisions of flowering plants. The magnoliids represent about 2 percent of all angiosperms and encompass around 8,500 species in twenty families. Its members are widespread throughout tropical and temperate regions of the world, taking various forms such as large trees, shrubs, vines, and occasionally herbs; some are large, economically important families such as Magnoliaceae, Lauraceae, Piperaceae, and Annonaceae. Many are known for their edible fruits, such as avocados (*Persea americana*), soursop (*Annona muricata*), and cherimoya (*Annona cherimola*). Spices such as black and white pepper (*Piper nigrum*), bay leaves (*Laurus nigrus*), nutmeg (*Myristica fragrans*), cinnamon (*Cinnamomum verum*), and camphor (*Cinnamomum camphora*) also belong to this clade. Other members are planted as ornamentals or used for timber.

ANNONACEAE (CUSTARD APPLES, SOURSOP)

This family consists of about 2,400 known species in 108 genera and is the largest family in the magnoliids. The family is primarily tropical in distribution, although some occur in mid-latitudes. They assume various forms, such as deciduous or evergreen trees, shrubs or lianas, some with aromatic bark, leaves, and flowers. Several genera are known for producing edible fruits, but only *Asimina triloba* (pawpaw) and *Annona glabra* (pond apple) are native to the United States. Pond apple is found only in Florida and the West Indies. Due to its limited shelf-life, our native pawpaw isn't commercially viable at this time, but researchers are working to develop strains that could be marketable in the future.

PAWPAW (AKA MISSOURI BANANA, HILLBILLY MANGO)
Asimina triloba

Native

Edible: ripe fruit

Many in the rural Ozarks are familiar with our native "Missouri banana." This tropical-looking native bears the largest fruit indigenous to North America. It has sweet, custard-like flesh with a flavor somewhere between banana, mango, and papaya. If not for its short shelf life, pawpaw might be on store shelves as our most popular native fruit!

Description

An understory shrub or tree to 30' tall, with smooth, splotched grayish bark, warty in older trees. Alternate leaves are 4"–12" long and 2"–4" across, medium-green with a pale under-surface, lanceolate to obovate, with smooth margins. Leaves produce a strong, unpleasant odor when crushed. Solitary, drooping flowers appear in March to early May before foliage appears; each is reddish or brownish purple, 1"–2" across, with three sepals, three inner petals, and three larger outer petals. Fruits are single or clustered, 3"–6" long, 1"–3" thick, green, maturing to brownish yellow with splotches. The ripe inner flesh is yellow, sur-rounding one or two rows of flattened, dark brown seeds up to ¾" long.

Habitat/Range

Found in shady, moist habitats, riparian areas, river bottoms, ravines, valleys, and bases of bluffs and slopes, often clonally spreading into large groves. Occurs in much of eastern North America, west to eastern Nebraska and Texas, north to Wisconsin, and New York into Ontario. Absent from most of New England.

Uses

Delicious peeled and eaten raw; can be baked, boiled into pudding, or added to breads or other dishes. Makes excellent jam and homemade ice cream. Because the pulp oxidizes quickly, add a bit of lemon juice to blended pulp and freeze in ice trays to preserve. Spread a thin layer of blended pulp on waxed paper and dry into fruit leather. To harvest, look for ground fall under the tree; a light shake of the trunk will bring down nearly ripe fruit. Hard, unripe fruits do not ripen well indoors; placing them in a paper bag with bananas can help. Leaves, twigs, and bark contain neurotoxic acetogenins that repel pests, so use crushed leaves as a handy insect repellent. The inner bark makes a strong cordage.

Warnings/Comments

Some people report contact dermatitis or allergic reactions to the entire plant. Pawpaw is a superfood packed with vitamins and minerals, exceeding apples, oranges, and bananas in essential amino acids. Compounds within the plant are under study to treat cancer. Some find the flavor of pawpaws distasteful, but I suspect they tasted one when past its prime—the flavor and odor can become cloyingly sweet and strong with age.

RECIPE

Pawpaw Pancakes with Wild Ginger / Spicebush Berry Butter Syrup

Use your favorite pancake recipe, and add ½ cup or so of diced pawpaw flesh.

Syrup:

2 cups brown sugar

1 cup water

½ cup butter

1 tablespoon each spicebush berries and wild ginger roots

Bring to a boil then simmer to desired thickness. Pour through a strainer. Use the left-over roots to make a crystalized wild ginger snack, as described in that plant's segment.

ARISTOLOCHIACEAE (BIRTHWORTS, PIPEVINES)

This family has 400 known species in seven genera, many of tropical origin. Several species are important as herbal medicines; a number are grown as ornamentals or curiosities. Some are extravagantly-flowered tropical vines, such as *Aristolochia elegans* (elegant Dutchman's pipe), and our native Dutchman's pipe, or pipevine (*A. macrophylla*), which is a host and food plant for the pipevine swallowtail butterfly (*Battus philenor*).

WILD GINGER
Asarum canadense

Native

Edible: roots

Description

A low-growing, early perennial with an inconspicuous flower. Paired, basal leaves are up to 3" long and 4" across, emerging from shallow, lateral rhizomes. Leaves are generally heart-shaped, with a deeply cleft base and a rounded tip, on hairy petioles up to 8" tall. They have a shiny, slightly pubescent upper surface, smooth margins, and conspicuous palmate veins. Blooms April–May. A single, hairy bud emerges from the paired leaf axil, maturing to a bell-shaped hollow calyx with three reddish-brown, pointed and decurved lobes.

Habitat/Range

Prefers rich soil and moist conditions. Found in bottomland and upland forest, bases of bluffs, moist valleys and ravines, banks and benches along streams and rivers. Range is throughout the eastern and midwestern United States and Canada, west to Oklahoma, Kansas, and the Dakotas.

Uses

Roots can be harvested throughout the year. Their strong flavor is reminiscent of commercial ginger root, which is an unrelated Asian species in the family Zingiberaceae. Use the roots fresh or dried as a ginger flavoring, or to make a pleasant tea. Boil them in a bit of brown sugar and water to make syrup; roll the leftover roots in confectioners' sugar and allow to dry for use as a snack or as crystallized ginger in cooked dishes and desserts. The flavored syrup can be served over desserts or pancakes; the flavor can be enhanced by the addition of a few spicebush berries or other good-flavored berries and plants. The root has antibacterial properties and can be used medicinally, externally as a poultice or internally for a number of ailments.

Warnings/Comments

Wild ginger and related plants can contain aristolochic acid, and could be toxic if eaten in quantity. To harvest sustainably, pinch or cut segments of root runners, leaving the rooted pairs of basal leaves intact to continue growth.

LAURACEAE (LAURELS)

This family consists of over 3,000 known species in about 52 genera, and its taxonomy is poorly understood. Many species are found in warm temperate or tropical habitats, and many are evergreen. Several species are deciduous, and a few are parasitic vines. The leaves, stems, and roots of most species in the laurel family are aromatic. The leaves are typically alternate, and the flowers are often small and yellow.

SPICEBUSH (AKA WILD ALLSPICE)
Lindera benzoin

Native

Edible: leaves, berries

Spicebush is one of my favorite plants! At every encounter while hiking, I can't resist grabbing a few spicebush leaves or twigs to nibble for the refreshing citrus-spice flavor.

Description

A branching understory shrub 6'–15' tall, occasionally with multiple stems, often forming colonies. Larger stem bark is brown to grayish brown, sparsely covered with round, whitish lenticels; smaller twig bark is shiny brown. Simple, alternate leaves are 2"–6" long, 1"–3" wide, light-green with pale undersides, with smooth margins and pointed tips.

Young leaves are oval; older leaves are ovate to obovate. Yellow fragrant flowers appear in March before leaves emerge; each is ¼" across, forming in clusters along branches. Fruit is a green, ovoid drupe about ½" long, maturing to bright, glossy red and fleshy in September–October. Each fruit contains a single, hard round seed. All parts of the plant are aromatic when crushed.

Habitat/Range

Found in partly to mostly shaded, damp habitats, in bottoms and low woodlands, bases of bluffs, along streambanks and spring branches, banks of shaded ponds, seeps, and along moist, forested roadsides. Will tolerate full sun when soil conditions are right. Range is throughout eastern North America, west to Texas and Iowa.

Uses

Young, tender raw leaves are a flavorful, citrusy addition to salads. Larger leaves can be added to other boiled greens and soups. Raw or dried leaves and fruits make a great summer tea, as do the twigs in winter. Fruits can be sparingly used raw for flavoring in syrups or sweets, or can be dried and ground as a substitute for allspice. Branches with leaves still attached can be broken off and used to pit-bake root vegetables, greens, and meats, baking flavor and moisture into the food. Start with a large, deep bed of coals. Scoop out a shallow pit 1½'–2' across, and layer the bottom with 2"–3" of leaves/branches. Add the food in the center, then cover with another layer of leaves/branches. Cover with larger glowing embers and burned stick ends; bake for 45–50 minutes. It's a great utensil-less cooking method for drier meats like venison or wild turkey breast and fall-apart meats like fish. This cooking method also works with other edible and flavorful leaves, such as sassafras, wild grape, and cut-leaved coneflower, but should only be used when the plants are encountered in abundance.

Warnings/Comments

Used internally and topically to treat various ailments. An important larval food plant for spicebush swallowtail butterflies and Promethea silkmoths. Planted as an ornamental in appropriate landscapes.

SASSAFRAS
Sassafras albidum

Native

Edible: leaves, leaf buds, roots

Digging sassafras root in March is practically a rite of spring in the Ozarks. It is used to make the beautiful, deep-red root-beer tea that is said to purify the blood after winter. No scientific evidence bears that out or has determined whether the blood even needs to be thinned, but the tea is still a delicious treat!

Description

Grows as a small to medium-size tree 30'–50', occasionally to 100', with a roughly ovoid crown, and irregular, contorted branches that turn upward. Trunk bark is gray-brown to reddish brown, with deep irregular furrows and flat-topped ridges. Young twigs and shoots are yellow-green and smooth, becoming brownish with gray lenticels with age. Alternate leaves are up to 6" long and 4" across, and have three distinct shapes: simple-ovoid, singly-lobed (mitten-shaped), and double-lobed (trident-shaped). All have smooth margins, rounded to slightly-pointed lobes, and are tapered at the base. Blooms April–May, with yellowish clusters of ⅓" flowers forming at the tips of branches. Flowers develop into ⅓" purplish, ovoid drupes on long, red stems that are swollen where the fruit attaches. All parts of the plant are aromatic.

Habitat/Range
Prefers mostly open habitats in a wide range of soil conditions. Found in open, dry woods and woodland borders, glades, prairies, fencerows, old fields, pastures, thickets, bluff openings, along roadsides and railroads. It is widely planted as an ornamental. Range is throughout the eastern United States and Ontario, west to Texas and Wisconsin.

Uses
Dig roots in late winter or early spring before leaf-out for excellent root-beer tea or jelly. Small roots can be used whole; use bark only of larger roots. Aboveground parts of the plant have a citrusy flavor with a slightly mucilaginous quality. Young, raw leaves and tender shoots are an excellent addition to salads. Dried leaves can be ground into powder to make a great stew flavoring/thickener, commonly used as gumbo seasoning, and is sold commercially as "gumbo filé." Leaf buds can be eaten raw or pickled and used as capers. Twigs can be used as aromatic toothpicks or chewed for flavor while hiking.

Warnings/Comments
As with all roots, never dig unless found in abundance. Commercial sale of the root was banned by the FDA in 1960, because its compound safrole, responsible for most of the root's unique flavor, was also determined to be carcinogenic. Laboratory rats developed liver tumors when injected with large doses or when fed a concentration of the isolated compound for long periods, but no evidence revealed harmful effects in humans. To be safe, store it where rats can't get to it.

EUDICOTS
(Formerly DICOTS)

Eudicots are the largest and most diverse group of the three main divisions of angiosperms, composing nearly 75 percent of all species of flowering plants. They are the most evolutionary advanced plants on Earth and assume a large number of forms, including tiny herbs, large vines, and giant trees. Their adaptability has allowed them to dominate the majority of land-based ecosystems in biomass and number of species across a huge variety of habitats. They are characterized as having two cotyledons in the seed, leaves with a network of veins radiating from a central main vein, flower parts in multiples of four or five, and a root system composed of a taproot or rootlets.

ADOXACEAE (MUSKROOTS, ELDERBERRIES, VIBURNUMS, MOSCHATELS)

This small family of flowering plants consists of 5 genera and about 150 to 200 species, including both woody-stemmed and herbaceous species. Most have flat-topped inflorescences composed of numerous small flowers that mature to produce fleshy drupes.

Elderberry in bloom, with elderberry fruits

COMMON ELDERBERRY (AKA BLACK ELDERBERRY)
Sambucus canadensis

Native

Edible: ripe berries only

A true superfood, elderberries are highly sought after by the health food market for their nutritious and antioxidant properties that help support the immune system. Studies show that elderberry juice may decrease cholesterol and reduce the level of fat in the blood, and their high anthocyanin content has been found to reduce the risk of heart disease. The berries can be used in a number of ways; my favorite is elderberry-infused moonshine. (Thanks, Howie!)

Description

A deciduous, colony-forming shrub up to 10' tall, often with multiple, arching stems that branch toward the top. Older stems have rough, grayish-brown bark with large, raised lenticels. Branches and twigs are grayish to yellowish brown, often smooth but occasionally ridged, with sparse lenticels. Young stems can be weak and brittle due to the prominent pith center. Shiny, dark green opposite leaves grow along stems and branches, each is 6"–12" long, odd-pinnately compound, with 2–4 opposite pairs of leaflets and one terminal leaflet. Leaflets are lanceolate to ovoid, 2"–6" long, 1"–2" wide, with serrated margins. Flat or dome-shaped snowy-white flower clusters up to 10" across form late May–July, emerging on umbel-like panicles at the tips of branches; individual ¼" flowers are 4-petaled. Fruiting heads mature August–October to bear numerous shiny round, purplish-black berries that are ¼" across, each containing 4 seeds.

Habitat/Range

Occurs in bottomland or mesic upland forests and their borders, prairies, thickets, streambanks, old fields, gardens; near ponds, lakes, seeps; pastures; disturbed ground along roadsides, railroads, and power line cuts. Range is the eastern United States, west to eastern Texas, north to eastern Nebraska.

Uses

Raw, ripe berries are edible, but flavor is improved somewhat by cooking. Use raw berries to make elderberry-infused brandy, moonshine, or vinegar. Cooked berries are great in pies and other confections, or can be used for syrup, jelly, and wine. Dried berries can be added to pancakes, muffins, sweet breads, and other sweet dishes. Fresh flowers can be added to breads, pancakes, and salads; fried in a light batter as fritters; used fresh or dried to make tea or fermented to make "elderflower champagne." To harvest berries, collect the entire fruiting heads and freeze; shake over a tarp or newspapers while still frozen to easily remove berries from stems. Soak berries in water to remove leftover stems, debris, and unripe berries. Various parts of the plant are used extensively as internal or external medicine for a number of ailments. Recent studies confirm that compounds from elderberries directly inhibit the flu virus's entry and replication in human cells, helping strengthen a person's immune response to the virus.

Warning/Comments

The root, stems, leaves, and unripe berries contain toxic cyanide-forming glycosides. Only consume ripe berries, taking care to clean out stems and unripe berries. Several cultivar species with higher fruit yields are planted commercially.

RECIPE

Elderflower Champagne

8 medium–large elderberry flower heads

1 gallon cold water

1 lemon, juiced, and its quartered skin

1½ pounds white sugar

3 tablespoons white wine vinegar

1. Dissolve sugar in a bit of the water, warmed and allowed to cool.

2. Mix the dissolved sugar with the other ingredients and the remaining water in a large jug or covered crock; leave covered in a cool place for 4 days.

3. Strain and pour into clean screw-top glass or plastic bottles; leave at ambient room temperature for another 4–10 days.

4. Test after a few days to make sure the mixture isn't over-carbonated, and check the bottles frequently by gently unscrewing the lid every few days to decompress. (They may explode if left unattended too long.) **Note:** Cooler environments may require more time to ferment, as the natural yeast in the flowers is doing the work and may take a while to get going. The longer the "champagne" ferments, the higher the alcohol content.

5. When it is fermented to your preference, refrigerate to slow down further fermentation.

BLACKHAW (AKA WILD RAISIN)
Viburnum prunifolium, V. rufidulum

Native

Edible: berries

Blackhaws are a sought-after treat during fall walks in the Ozarks, along with persimmons, wild grapes, wild plums, farkleberries, and other late-fruiting plants. Some fruits dry on the plant and resemble raisins, providing foraging opportunities well into the early-winter months.

Description

A stiff-branched, woody shrub or small tree to 25'. Dark green, opposite leaves up to 3" long and 1" across form on short green to reddish petioles. They are ovate to obovate in shape, with finely serrated margins. Bark is gray to reddish brown and rough on small branches, becoming furrowed into plates on older trees. White blooms develop in cymes up to 5" across that emerge from the leaf axil in April–May, each with numerous 5-petaled ¼" flowers. In September–October, flowers mature to produce blue-black ½" ovoid drupes, each with sweet flesh covering a flattened hard seed. *V. rufidium* (rusty blackhaw) is similar, but with smaller, glossy, leathery leaves on rusty-red petioles and a more restricted range.

Habitat/Range

Found in rocky woodlands and hillsides, forest edges, streambanks, roadsides, glades, thickets, above and below bluffs. Distributed throughout the southeastern United States, north to the Great Lakes, west to Texas and Kansas, south to the Gulf Coast except Florida, and east to Connecticut and the mid-Atlantic states.

Uses

Ripe fruits are great as a raisin-type trail snack, often drying on the stem and persisting into winter. They are good for jam. Or make a beverage by soaking, mashing, and occasionally agitating the fruits in a jar of hot water to dissolve the flesh; strain to remove skin and seeds.

Warnings/Comments

Blackhaws are commonly planted as an attractive ornamental shrub; the leaves turn lavender or bright red in the fall, and the fruits attract birds and wildlife. *V. dentatum* (southern arrowwood) grows bunches of long, straight stems, and is preferred for arrow making. *Viburnum* leaves, bark, and root bark were used extensively by Native Americans for medicinal purposes. The plant contains several powerful compounds, including a type of the blood thinner coumarin and salicin, a natural form of aspirin. Those with a reaction to aspirin should avoid using the plant medicinally.

AMARANTHACEAE (AMARANTHS, GOOSEFOOTS)

This large family of herbs and shrubs is distributed worldwide, and consists of roughly 2,040 species in 165 genera. It includes the former goosefoot family, Chenopodiaceae, making it the most species-rich lineage within its parent order, Caryophyllales. Some members are economically important food crops such as beets and quinoa, and several are cultivated as garden ornamentals.

COMMON AMARANTH (AKA REDROOT, ROUGH PIGWEED)
Amaranthus retroflexus

Introduced

Edible: shoots, leaves, seeds

Known as the "Grain of the Aztecs" and steeped in pre-Hispanic Mexican history, amaranth seeds and greens were diet staples in ancient Mesoamerica. The seed flour was predominant in the culture, to the point that it was fashioned into images of gods and eaten as communion. This so offended the religious sensibilities of the Christian Europeans during their colonization of Mexico that it led to a total ban on the natives' cultivation of the plant. Amaranth grain has recently become popular as a gluten-free and super-nutritious wheat alternative.

Description

A weedy annual 1'–3' tall, with a hairy, branched central stem terminating in bristly flower spikes. Alternate, simple leaves are on petioles, ovate to elliptic, up to 6" long and 4" across, becoming smaller as they ascend the stem. Leaf margins are smooth or slightly wavy; veins appear as grooves. In late summer

Amaranth seeds

the stems and branches produce a flowering panicle of bristly pale green or purple spikes up to 6" long, with shorter spikes forming at the leaf axil. As the spikes dry, they release prodigious amounts of tiny, flattened-roundish tan or black seeds.

Purple and green seed heads

Habitat/Range

Prefers disturbed, open habitats. Found in gardens, barnyards, pastures, croplands, old fields, roadsides, and waste areas. Native to the tropical Americas, naturalized throughout the United States and Canada. Widely cultivated for culinary uses in Eurasia and other countries.

RECIPE

Alegria

2 cups popped amaranth seeds

Small amount of toasted, crushed pepitas or nuts

Small amount of chopped dried fruit

Dash of cinnamon or similar spice

3 tablespoons honey

1. Mix dry ingredients in a pan on low heat; add honey slowly till it thins a bit and binds to other ingredients.

2. Place a sheet of parchment paper on a flat tray; spread the mix evenly while slightly pressing with another sheet of parchment to bind everything together. Let cool till it hardens.

3. Cut into bars and serve.

Uses

Young shoots, tender tops, and leaves can be added raw to salads or cooked as a potherb. Use it as you would its cousin, spinach. The nutritious seeds can be sprouted, cooked as a cereal, or popped and used in a sweet confection called alegria (Spanish for "happiness"). Seeds can be roasted and ground into flour for making tortillas, muffins, cakes, and breads or used to make beverages such as atole (a warm beverage usually made with corn masa) or beer. To harvest, twist and work the fully dried flower spikes inside a plastic bag to release the seeds, then winnow the remaining dried bracts by bowl-to-bowl (or hand-to-hand) pouring while blowing through it, or by pouring in front of a fan on low setting. Too much air will also blow away the tiny seeds. A flour sifter speeds the process, as most of the seeds will fall through the wire mesh. What remains can be further bowl- or hand-winnowed till clean.

Warnings/Comments

This and related species contain high levels of oxalic acid, and should be avoided by those suffering from kidney stones and related ailments. *A. spinosus* (spiny amaranth) is similar, but with narrower leaves and spiny stems. Most *Amaranthus* species can become agricultural pests.

LAMB'S QUARTER (AKA WHITE GOOSEFOOT)
Chenopodium album

Introduced

Edible: shoots, leaves, seeds

Spinach is the most well-known and widely cultivated member of this family. The seeds of the South American species *C. quinoa* were considered to be sacred, and the plant was so heavily utilized that it was called "the Mother of all Grains." It has recently become popular as a gluten-free alternative to wheat, sold commercially as the Incan grain quinoa.

Description

A weedy annual 1'–6' tall, usually branched, with a bushy appearance. Stem is smooth and angular, pale green, developing purplish linear stripes with age. Alternate leaves are varied, up to 5" long, 3" wide, either diamond-shaped, triangular, or lanceolate, with lobed or dentate margins on larger leaves. Leaf undersides and young stems have a white, mealy coating. Minute green flowers form in small clusters along spikes at leaf axils and the end of stems, sometimes becoming reddish at maturity. The ovary of each flower produces a flattened, somewhat round, black seed; one plant can produce up to 75,000 seeds.

Habitat/Range

A disturbed-ground invader found in mostly open habitats, pastures, cropland, gardens, old fields, vacant lots, and waste areas; occurs throughout North America. Native to Europe and Asia; its origins are unclear, as it has naturalized globally due to anthropogenic distribution and cultivation.

Uses

Young, raw leaves are excellent in salads; older leaves can be boiled, steamed, and used in soups or other cooked dishes. Use it in any way you would use spinach. The seeds can be sprouted, ground for flour, or added to other ground plant seeds such as curly dock, amaranth, or climbing false buckwheat to make crackers or seed cakes. The whitish dust on the undersides of the leaves is made of mineral salts from the soils and can be used as a nutritious salt replacement or used to flavor other plants. The entire plant can be pulled when in seed and hung upside down to dry. When thoroughly dried, strip the foliage and seeds for use in soups and other cooked dishes, or grind for use as a flour additive or soup thickener.

Warnings/Comments

Many plants in this family contain a high amount of oxalic acid and should be consumed sparingly, or avoided entirely by those suffering from kidney stones and related ailments. The leaves are quite variable in flavor from one plant to another; a taste test will help you pick the tastiest individuals before harvesting.

ANACARDIACEAE (CASHEWS, SUMACS)

This family consists of 83 genera with about 860 known species. Many members bear fruits that are drupes, including economically important species such as cashew, mango, and pistachio. Some members produce the skin irritant urushiol, found in poison ivy, oak, and sumac.

SMOOTH SUMAC (AKA RED SUMAC, SHOEMAKE)
Rhus glabra

Native

Edible: shoots, berries
The health benefits alone of sumac berries should make them a list-topper for foragers. High levels of antioxidants and vitamin C give it superfood status, and it has a nice, tart flavor to boot!

Description

A colony-forming shrub to 15' tall, with leafy branches near the top of the stems. Bark is smooth and reddish brown on young plants, becoming grayish brown with raised horizontal lenticels. Trunk bark on older plants becomes slightly grooved. Alternate, compound leaves are odd-pinnate with 9–25 leaflets, forming on long, purplish stalks with a whitish coating. Each leaflet is 4½" long to 1" wide, narrowly lanceolate, with shallow, toothed margins, a pale to dark green upper surface, and pale to white undersides. In late May–July, clusters of small white or pale green flowers form on erect panicles up to 10" long at the stem terminus. Female flowers mature August–September into Christmas tree–shaped tight clusters of small, red to dark maroon drupes. Stems and leaves exude a white latex when broken, and the leaves turn brilliant orange or red in fall.

Habitat/Range
Prefers open or disturbed habitats. Occurs in thickets, prairies, glades, fencerows, old fields, woodland borders and openings, and along roadsides and railroads. Range is throughout the continental United States and Canada.

Uses
Tender shoots can be peeled and eaten raw or cooked; harvest when the inside is solid green, before the whitish pith forms. For awesome sumac lemonade, fill a gallon jar half-full of fresh seed heads and cover with hot water; agitate berries periodically to release flavor. Strain through a cheesecloth and sweeten to taste. Berries are best harvested early, before the waxy, tart coating loses flavor. Berries can be used for jelly, added to salads and soups; or used as a topping for any dish requiring a tart or lemony element. Dried, ground berries make a colorful, superior meat rub or seasoning for any dish. It is very popular in Middle Eastern cuisine, known there as za'atar. The dried leaves can be used in smoking mixtures. Pithy stems can be hollowed out for use as pipestems, blowtubes, or spiles for tapping syrup trees. All parts of the plant are used medicinally for a number of ailments.

Warnings/Comments
Plants in this family can produce contact dermatitis in some, especially *Toxicodendron radicans* (poison ivy), *T. pubescens* (poison oak), and *T. vernix* (poison sumac). Poison sumac has similar leaves and structure to compound-leaved *Rhus* species, but it has white berries clustered along the stem instead of terminal red clusters, and does not occur in the Ozarks. There are four species of *Rhus* in the Ozarks. *R. copallinum* (winged sumac) is similar to *R. glabra* but has a winged leaf rachis. *R. typhis* (staghorn sumac) grows to 30' and has reddish hairs on the upper stem and berries. *R. aromatica* (fragrant sumac) has aromatic, trifoliate leaves and small clusters of hairy red berries.

Sumac and Gooseberry Margarita

1 cup sweetened sumac lemonade

1½ ounces tequila

1 ounce triple sec or other orange liqueur

Crushed gooseberries or other wild berries or fruits (Add an extra dash of agave nectar or stevia if using gooseberries.)

Muddle fruits in a large glass. Add other ingredients; stir well and serve over ice in a salt/sugar-rimmed cocktail glass. Optional flavorings include wild fruit syrups such as prickly pear, any species of sweet berry, or savory herbs. This drink pairs well with grilled prickly pear tacos.

Fragrant sumac

APIACEAE (CARROTS, PARSLEY)

This large family has 3,700 species in 434 genera, including some of our most well-known domestic plants such as parsley, celery, coriander, cumin, dill, fennel, caraway, and parsnips. It also contains extremely toxic plants such as poison hemlock and water hemlock.

SPREADING CHERVIL
Chaerophyllum procumbens

Native

Edible: young leaves, stems and seeds

Description

This inconspicuous spring annual is usually under 1' tall, with several weak, branching stems that often sprawl or lean on adjacent vegetation. The stems are shiny, green to purplish green, with small hairs in lateral lines or in tufts where stems branch. Alternate leaves are up to 4" long and 2" across, double-pinnate, and triangular to lanceolate in shape, with a papery sheath around the petiole. Leaflets are pinnatifid, deeply to shallowly lobed, and feathery in appearance. In late spring, small umbellate clusters of 3–7 flowers appear at the terminus of stems and branches and at leaf axils. Individual flowers are white, 5-petaled, and less than 1/8" across, each maturing to oblong seeds about ¼" long.

Habitat/Range

Occurs in partially shaded conditions in moist, rich soil, in mesic forests, open woodlands and their borders, bluffs, thickets, glades, near buildings, and along streambanks, roads, and railroads. Range is mostly eastern United States, west to Oklahoma and Nebraska, north to the Great Lakes states. Absent from New England.

Uses

Young tender leaves are a nice spring salad ingredient or potherb, with a slight anise-celery flavor. Some sources report that the plant has a disagreeable taste, but that's not my experience. Seeds can be used for seasoning.

Warnings/Comments

The introduced *Anthriscus sylvestris* (wild chervil, cow parsley) is a cultivated vegetable in Europe but is rarely found in the Ozarks. No member of Apiaceae should be consumed without 100 percent positive identification.

CANADIAN HONEWORT
Cryptotaenia canadensis

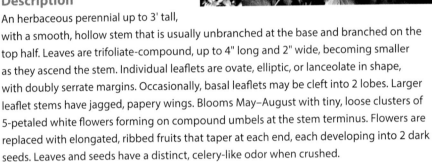

Edible: all parts

This savory wild edible is often over-looked, but it is always a tasty addition to salads and cooked greens.

Description
An herbaceous perennial up to 3' tall, with a smooth, hollow stem that is usually unbranched at the base and branched on the top half. Leaves are trifoliate-compound, up to 4" long and 2" wide, becoming smaller as they ascend the stem. Individual leaflets are ovate, elliptic, or lanceolate in shape, with doubly serrate margins. Occasionally, basal leaflets may be cleft into 2 lobes. Larger leaflet stems have jagged, papery wings. Blooms May–August with tiny, loose clusters of 5-petaled white flowers forming on compound umbels at the stem terminus. Flowers are replaced with elongated, ribbed fruits that taper at each end, each developing into 2 dark seeds. Leaves and seeds have a distinct, celery-like odor when crushed.

Habitat/Range
Found in moist, rich woodlands, bottoms, slopes, ravines, springs, seeps, and bases of bluffs. Occurs throughout eastern North America and Canada, west to Texas and the Dakotas.

Uses
Tender, aboveground parts are a good celery-flavored addition to salad greens and can be added to potherb greens and other cooked dishes. As with nettles and other greens, the boil water makes a nutritious soup stock. Young shoots and even older stems are excellent when steamed or sautéed. Seeds can be used as a seasoning. Roots are small and occasionally tough, but they are tasty when sautéed in butter or boiled.

Warnings/Comments
In early growth, honewort could possibly be confused with slightly toxic *Ranunculus* (buttercup) or *Sanicula* (sanicle) species at first glance. A smell test and attention to detail with identification will separate it from other similar edible or nonedible plants. *C. japonica* is cultivated as a vegetable in Japan.

WILD CARROT (AKA QUEEN ANNE'S LACE)
Daucus carota

Introduced

Edible: roots, leaves, seeds (See "Warnings/Comments.")

Description
This familiar biennial wildflower forms a basal rosette from a tap root during the first year, and produces a branching, flowering stalk up to 5' tall the second year. Alternate, compound leaves are up to 10" long, fernlike, and bipinnately divided into narrow segments, becoming shorter and sparser as they ascend the hairy stem. Blooms May–October. Flower heads are compound umbels forming at the stem terminus, generally round and flat-topped or domed, up to 5" across. They are densely packed with tiny, white 5-petaled flowers, often with a small purple flower at the center. The flowers mature to small, elongated bristly seeds. As the flower head becomes concave, seeds eventually fall into the bottom of the dried cup-shaped structure.

Habitat/Range
Found in open, disturbed habitats, pastures, old fields, tops of bluffs, glades, fencerows, roadsides, railroads, yards, gardens, and vacant lots. Native to Eurasia, naturalized across the United States and Canada.

Uses
The root has a distinctive carrot smell and can be used like a domestic carrot. Young, first-year roots are good raw in salads or can be cooked in soups and other dishes. Second-year roots become tough and woody, but the fleshy outer part can be boiled in soups for flavor. Small amounts of young, tender leaves can be chopped and added raw to salads or can be added to other cooked greens. Flower heads can be fried in batter as fritters. Seeds are a good seasoning and are often present in the dried flower heads throughout winter.

Poison hemlock vs. wild carrot

Warnings/Comments

The extremely toxic *Conium maculatum* (poison hemlock) has been misidentified as wild carrot, occasionally with fatal results. Second-year flowering plants are easily differentiated; poison hemlock has smooth purple-spotted hollow stems, chambered roots, and compound umbels that are more widely spaced than wild carrot. It also has larger, more robust leaves and does not smell like carrot. (See "Poisonous Plants" for full description.) Identification can be more difficult while collecting in early spring; when they are both emerging, they can appear quite similar. Do not depend on the carrot smell if you've already harvested carrot; you may have the smell on your hands and think it is coming from the hemlock root. DO NOT consume unless identification is 100 percent positive! Many sources advise to avoid all members of the family until identified by an expert (see image of hemlock versus wild carrot). The smaller native *D. pusillus* (American wild carrot) is present but uncommon in the Ozarks, its range limited to southern portions of the United States.

ANISEROOT (AKA SWEET CICELY, SWEETROOT)
Osmorhiza longistylus

Native

Edible: all parts

This is another great edible I discovered from the habit of smell-testing unknown plants. It quickly became a favorite addition to salads after I learned more about it.

Description
An herbaceous perennial to 3' tall, with delicate fernlike leaves on slightly hairy branching stems. Alternate leaves are smooth to slightly hairy; leaflets are twice ternately compound with the terminal leaf usually larger than sub-leaves, all with blunt-toothed margins. Lower compound leaves are up to 9" long and 9" wide, becoming smaller as they ascend the stem. Blooms April–June, with flowers appearing in compound umbels at the stem terminus. Each umbel is typically composed of about 5 umbellets, each umbellet having 8–16 tiny white flowers. Each flower has 5 petals, 5 white-tipped stamens, and 2 white styles, which exceed the length of the petals. Fruit is long and narrow with stiff hairs, splitting lengthwise into two slender black seeds with barbed tips connected at tip. Roots are carrot-like, small and white. All parts of the plant have a pleasant, anise-like aroma.

Habitat/Range
Found in rich soil conditions in mesic to moist woodlands, wooded valleys, slopes, bottoms, ravines, and along streambanks. Range is all of eastern United States except Louisiana and Florida, west to the Rocky Mountain states.

Uses
Raw, all tender aboveground parts are a great trail nibble, or they can be added to green or fruit salads, cooked dishes, and soups as a fennel substitute. The raw or cooked root has a sweet, carrot-like flavor with a hint of anise; it can be eaten raw, steamed, pit-baked, or added to other dishes. The seeds are good for seasoning. As with all natives, collect sparingly, and do not dig roots unless encountered in abundance.

Warnings/Comments
Numerous *Osmorhiza* species in the United States and the plant *Myrrhis odorata* are all referred to as sweet cicely, and all are edible. The Ozarks are also home to *O. claytonii* (woolly sweet cicely), which is found mostly north of the Missouri River. Its anise flavor is slightly less intense than *O. longistylus*. A smell test to detect the scent of anise will separate *Osmorhiza* species from look-alikes.

APOCYNACEAE (MILKWEEDS)

This family of 415 genera and about 4,600 species of trees, shrubs, woody vines, and herbs is found mostly in tropical and subtropical areas of the world. Members of the family have milky, often toxic juice, smooth-margined leaves, and flowers in clusters. Our native milkweeds are in the subfamily Asclepiadoideae; most have showy flowers and seedpods that split to release tufted seeds.

COMMON MILKWEED
Asclepias syriaca

Native

Edible: shoots, leaves, flower buds, seedpods

Description

An erect perennial up to 6', with a single, stout stem that branches near the top when flower clusters form. Opposite, petioled leaves are up to 7" long, broadly elliptical, with a prominent central vein and smooth margins. Fragrant blooms appear May–August; umbellate flower clusters up to 4½" across form on pedicels at leaf axils and at the stem terminus. Individual flowers are ¼" across, light pink to pale purple, each with 5 recurved petals and 5 erect, curved hoods. Teardrop-shaped seedpods grow to 4" long, covered with soft, slender projections. All parts exude a white, milky latex when torn.

Habitat/Range

Found in mostly open habitats in prairies, pastures, roadsides, fencerows, woodland borders, old fields, and disturbed waste areas. Occurs over most of the central and eastern United States and in Canada.

Milkweed flower and shoot

Milkweed pods at collection stage

Uses

Young, tender shoots, leaves, flower buds, and small seedpods are good after boiling; some compare the flavor to okra, without the slime. Larger pods are dry and unpalatable. Older references say the latex sap is bitter until cooked off, but I've found that the topmost paired leaves on younger plants are pretty tasty raw as a trail nibble. I've had them many times and have yet to find a bitter one. The fibrous outer skin of the stem makes good cordage. The dry seed fluff is good clothing insulation or fire-starter, and the latex is said to be good for removing warts.

Warnings/Comments

Avoid narrow-leaved milkweed species; they can be fairly toxic. Do not consume if any bitterness persists after cooking. Native milkweeds are a critical host plant of monarch butterflies, so collect sparingly. There are at least 17 species of *Asclepias* in the Ozarks.

ASTERACEAE (ASTERS, SUNFLOWERS, COMPOSITE-FLOWERED PLANTS)

This family has cosmopolitan distribution, and includes over 32,000 species in more than 1,900 genera. It is rivaled only by Orchidaceae in number of species, and may represent up to 10 percent of all native flora in any given region. The bewildering number of similar species can make identification so difficult that some use the term "DYC" (damned yellow composites) to describe certain groups. Many species have both ray florets and disk florets; some may have only one or the other. Asteraceae contains many plants that are grown commercially for gardens, and several economically important species such as lettuce, endive, artichokes, and sunflowers. A few species such as dandelions, ragweed, and thistles are considered to be noxious pests in lawns, gardens and agricultural areas.

HORSEWEED (AKA MARE'S TAIL)
Conyza canadensis

Native

Edible: shoots, leaves, flower buds

Description

Horseweed, before flowering

A stout-stemmed annual with a single, hairy stem; densely arranged alternate leaves occurring along the length of the stem, giving it a whorled and weedy appearance. On large specimens, the stem may branch profusely in the uppermost part during flowing. Individual leaves are elliptic or narrowly lanceolate, 2"–3½" long and ¼"–½" across, growing smaller as they ascend the stem. Lower, larger leaves may have sparsely dentate margins, upper stem leaves are typically smaller with smooth margins, and both have conspicuous hairs along their edges. Blooms June–November, with numerous small flowers forming on a large panicle at the stem terminus, often with smaller panicles emerging at the upper leaf axils. The panicle stems develop leaflike bracts up to 1" long. Individual flowers are about ¼" long, urn-shaped, with tiny, inconspicuous petaloid rays.

Habitat/Range

Found commonly in open, disturbed habitats, in pastures, vacant lots, fencerows, gardens, prairies, glades, openings in upland forests, and along roadsides and streambanks. Range is throughout the United States and southern provinces of Canada.

Uses

Young, tender leaves have a fairly strong flavor and can be added sparingly to salads or used to spice up other dishes. They are excellent when dried and ground for a seasoning similar to tarragon. Young shoots and leaves can be boiled as a potherb. Flower buds and tender tops can be pulverized and added to cooked dishes. The dried stem is one of the best materials from which to make a hand-drill spindle for a friction fire.

Warnings/Comments

Horseweed is a serious agricultural pest, especially in corn and soybean fields. It was one of the first plants to develop a resistance to glyphosate, first recorded in 2001 in Delaware. The genus contains around 167 accepted species, with several that are quite similar to *C. canadensis*. Similar species with hairless stems are uncommon.

COMMON BURDOCK (AKA LESSER BURDOCK)
Arctium minus

Introduced

Edible: shoots, petioles, roots

Description

A large-leaved biennial that forms a first-year basal rosette from a taproot; branched flowering stems emerge the second year. Basal leaves are ovate to broadly cordate, up to 2' long and 1½' across, with a dull green upper surface, wavy margins, and pale, woolly undersides. Petioles are long and hollow, usually furrowed along the top surface. Flowering stems are often hollow and up to 6' tall, ridged and hairy, later becoming smooth and with prominent longitudinal veins. Leaves on flowering stems are alternate, usually smaller than basal leaves. Flowers appear June–October, clustered on racemes at the stem terminus or at the leaf axil. Each flower is a globe-shaped involucre covered in bracts that terminate in hooked spines ¾"–1" across, with tubular, pale lavender or purple corollas and white, elongated styles. These flower heads dry out to become burs that catch on passing animals or humans for seed distribution.

A good-size burdock root

Habitat/Range

Common in barnyards, pastures, old fields, thickets, fencerows, woodland and cropland borders, power line cuts, and roadsides. Prefers disturbed, open ground but can colonize paths and animal trails in woodlands. Native to Eurasia; naturalized throughout the United States and Canada.

Burdock shoot at collection stage

Uses

Young, first-year roots can be eaten raw, slow-roasted, boiled, or fried. Older first-year roots can be peeled of their bitter exterior and boiled or added to soups. Young shoots of flower stems can be peeled and cooked as a vegetable. Pre-flowering older stems can be parboiled then peeled and cooked if they aren't too tough. Petioles of basal rosette leaves can be cooked as a vegetable. The root was combined with dandelion leaves and other ingredients to make beer. The root is also known for its immune-building, antioxidant, and aphrodisiac properties. Studies on burdock seeds have shown positive results for treating tumors and other cancers.

Warnings/Comments

Cultivars with larger, fleshier roots are grown in Japan for culinary use known as gobo. Two similar introduced species, *A. lappa* (great burdock) and *A. tomentosum* (woolly burdock), are found in the United States but are less common. In 1941 the Swiss inventor George de Mestral noticed the hooked spines of burdock seeds imbedded in his dog's fur and used the idea to invent a fastener he later patented as Velcro.

RECIPE

Southern-Fried Burdock Shoots

2–3 young burdock shoots, peeled and sliced into 3"–4" pieces

I tablespoon olive oil

1 egg, beaten

1 cup or more 50/50 mix of corn starch and unbleached flour

Salt and pepper to taste

Select only tender shoots; tough shoots will be harder to cut. Harvest by cutting close to the ground, then trim the leaf stalks. The inside of the stalk should be solid; if a hole appears in the center, it may be too tough. Peel by using a paring knife to grab and strip off the tough skin; slice away any remaining parts that appear to have grooves. (**Note:** If it will be a while before the shoots are cooked, add a bit of lemon juice to keep them from oxidizing and turning brown.)

1. Boil shoots in salted water for 3–5 minutes; remove.

2. Put shoots in a bowl with the egg; remove and roll them in the flour mixture.

3. Place in a skillet with the hot oil; fry until brown.

A half root is often all you get in our rocky soil.

RECIPE

Kinpira Gobo (Asian Stir-fried Burdock Root)

2 pounds peeled burdock root, sliced thin diagonally (Cover with water until ready to cook.)

¼ pound carrots, peeled and cut into short, thin strips

1½ teaspoons mirin (sweet rice wine)

1 tablespoon sugar

½ tablespoon sake

1 tablespoon soy sauce

1 teaspoon sesame seeds

2 tablespoons vegetable oil

1. Put the burdock roots into a skillet with the hot oil. Cook for a couple minutes and stir in the carrots.

2. Add the mirin, sugar, and sake; cook until the liquid is gone.

3. Mix in the soy sauce and cook till tender. Serve topped with sesame seeds.

Native tall thistle, showing white leaf undersurface

TALL THISTLE (AKA MEADOW THISTLE, ROADSIDE THISTLE)
Cirsium altissimum

Native

Edible: shoots, young leaves, peeled stems, seeds

I learned about this plant from a Cherokee elder in Georgia during his river cane blowgun class. A dart was made from a sliver of cane, and thistle seed head fluff was spun onto the end with string for fletching. The bonus was learning that peeled, the young thistle stems were delicious!

Description

A biennial or perennial with spiny leaves, erect stems to 8', and showy, purplish-pink flowers. First-year plants form a basal rosette; flower stalks emerge the second year. Main stems and branches are sparsely hairy, sometimes woolly-pubescent, with longitudinal ridges. Alternate leaves are up to 8" long and 3" across, generally lanceolate to elliptic, with a sparsely-haired upper surface and white, woolly undersides, becoming smaller as they ascend the stem. Margins are usually dentate to lobed and spiny, occasionally smooth with prickles. Numerous blooms appear July–October, forming singly at the ends of upper branches. Flowers are up to 2" across, with multitudes of disk florets in a bulb-shaped head, each with 5 pink, tubular corollas. The flowers dry into brown seed heads, opening to expose a fluffy bundle of numerous white pappus bristles attached to small, bullet-shaped seeds for wind distribution.

Bull thistle peeled stem

Habitat/Range
Found commonly along roadsides, in pastures, power line cuts, prairies, glades, old fields, streambanks, bases of bluffs, open bottomlands, upland forest openings and borders. Range is the eastern and midwestern United States, west to North Dakota and Texas. Absent from New England.

Uses
All true thistles are edible. Young shoots are great as a potherb. Cut lower segments of young stems at the ground and peel for a crunchy, celery-like field nibble. Roots of basal rosettes can be eaten raw or cooked or used in soups. Young leaves can be cooked as a potherb; the small spines soften with cooking. Trim the spines on larger leaves. The center section and midrib can be eaten raw or cooked. Seeds can be roasted and ground for an additive to flour or seedcakes. Some sources report that unopened thistle flower buds can be steamed or roasted, the soft parts pushed out of the calyx like an artichoke heart. My experiments of trying this with our native species resulted in a small bit of fibrous and unpalatable fluff, even when the buds were collected at a very early stage. All parts of the plant have been used medicinally.

Warnings/Comments
Introduced species such as *C. vulgare* (bull thistle) and related species like *Carduus nutans* (musk thistle) are considered noxious weeds, so it's best to avoid spreading seeds. Nine species of *Cirsium* occur in the Ozarks. *C. discolor* (field thistle) is a similar native that can interbreed with *C. altissimum*.

JERUSALEM ARTICHOKE
(Spoiler: It's neither an artichoke nor from Jerusalem!)
Helianthus tuberosus

Native

Edible: tubers

During a wilderness skills class, my assistant decided to include the starchy tubers of a newly discovered patch of Jerusalem artichoke in nearly every meal we ate. Their high inulin content must have fueled epic gas production, because that night we reenacted the campfire scene in the film *Blazing Saddles*! They are called "fartichokes" for good reason.

Description

A showy perennial with a hairy, green to reddish-brown stem up to 12' tall, usually with multiple branches on the top half, and with yellow ray flowers forming on long peduncles at the stem terminus. Leaves are on ¼"–2" winged petioles, opposite at the stem base, becoming alternate as they ascend the stem. Leaf blades are up to 7" long and 4" across, lance-shaped to broadly ovate-acute, pubescent to hairy, with entire to broadly-toothed margins. Flower heads are typical of sunflowers, consisting of a central cluster of disk florets surrounded by 10–20 yellow ray florets, up to 3½" across. Tubers are irregular, round to elongated, up to 4" long and 2" across, and occasionally spread to form large colonies.

Jerusalem artichoke tubers

Range/Habitat
Found in rich, upland and bottomland forests, woodland borders, pastures, roadsides, fencerows, streambanks, pond edges, disturbed ground, and moist depressions in upland prairies. Range is throughout the United States and Canada. Absent from the desert Southwest and western Canadian provinces.

Uses
The tubers are somewhat sweet, nutty, and crunchy when eaten raw, and are a great addition to salads and other raw vegetable dishes. Can be cooked like potatoes: boiled, roasted, fried, or added to soups. They are also good for pickling. Best when harvested later in the year, when the indigestible polysaccharides have converted to digestible sugars. Pickling, or soaking and cooking in lemon juice, will also help degasify them.

Warnings/Comments
Large, cultivar varieties are sold commercially as "sunchokes." A variety of commercial bioproducts are derived from the tubers, including inulin, fructose, natural fungicides, bioethanol, and antioxidants used as food additives. Overconsumption can occasionally cause stomach distress, but normally results in nothing more than extreme flatulence. It's a plant that can provide both food AND campfire entertainment!

OXEYE DAISY (AKA COMMON DAISY)
Leucanthemum vulgare

Introduced

Edible: leaves, buds, flowers, roots
This common plant is familiar to almost everyone, but many aren't aware of its great herblike flavor. The leaves are a nice addition to salads when available.

Description

An herbaceous perennial up to 3'; the mostly unbranched, leaved stem emerges from a basal rosette. Basal and middle leaves are on petioles, 2"–6" long, dark green, ovate to spoon-shaped, with coarsely dentate or lobed margins. Alternate leaves on the stem are lanceolate and sessile, with sparse, bluntly-serrated margins, becoming smaller as they ascend stem. Blooms May–August. Flowers appear singly at the stem terminus, each with a yellow central disk and 20–30 radial, white ray florets up to 2" across.

Habitat/Range

Found primarily in open or disturbed ground, in pastures, fields, glades, prairies, roadsides, lawns, and open-canopy woodlands. Native to Europe and temperate Asia; naturalized throughout North America.

Uses

Raw, tender leaves, unopened buds, and young flowers have great flavor as a trail nibble; also great as salad ingredients or pizza toppings. Flower buds can be marinated or pickled and used as capers. Fresh or dried flowers make a nice herbal tea. Young roots can be eaten raw or cooked. The plant was used medicinally for centuries to treat a number of ailments; is said to have a calming effect like chamomile.

Warnings/Comments

Listed as a noxious weed in some states due to its aggressive, colonizing nature. Allergies and contact dermatitis have been reported from this plant but are extremely rare. A number of cultivars are commercially available for flower gardens.

CUT-LEAVED CONEFLOWER
(AKA GREEN-HEADED CONEFLOWER, SOCHAN)
Rudbeckia laciniata

Native

Edible: shoots, leaves

I'd heard or read for years about the Cherokee gathering sochan as one of their favorite spring greens. After learning that it was a common plant I knew as cut-leaved coneflower, I was hooked after sampling the first batch! It has a long collection period and is usually found near water, perfect for incorporating into your foraging forays.

Description

An herbaceous perennial 3'–9' tall, sometimes forming large colonies from spreading rhizomes. Large basal leaves are up to 12" long and 10" across, alternate, deeply lobed in 3–7 segments, sometimes pinnate with a pair of basal leaflets and a lobed terminal leaflet, becoming smaller and with fewer lobes as they ascend the branching stems. Upper leaves are lanceolate, lacking lobes, often on winged petioles. Blooms July–September; flowers are 2"–3" across, composite, with 6–12 drooping, yellow petals and a dome-shaped center disk. They form singly or on cyme-like clusters of 2" long stalks at the stem apex and tips of branches.

Habitat/Range

Found in moist soil conditions in floodplains, bottomland forests, streambanks, partially shaded sloughs, wet fields, ditches, seeps, and forest edges. Widespread over most of the United States and Canada. Absent from Oregon, Nevada, and California.

Cut-leaved coneflower leaf

Uses

This plant has a nice herb/celery flavor. Young, tender raw leaves are a great salad addition. Leaves and shoots are used as a potherb, collected when they first come up in the spring. Older, larger leaves can be cut up for boiled greens until they get too strong or too tough to eat.

Warnings/Comments

Some species of *Ranunculus* (buttercup family) may have somewhat similar foliage, but a taste test and attention to characteristics will easily differentiate the two. There are five recognized wild varieties of *R. laciniata*; many commercial cultivar varieties are available. Often planted in flower gardens, the flowers are a good nectar source for late pollinators such as butterflies and bumblebees.

ASTERACEAE, SUBFAMILY CICHORIEAE (DANDELION TRIBE)

A subfamily of Asteraceae, this tribe is home to many edible species, although some tend to the bitter side of the flavor spectrum. All exude a milky latex when torn or broken.

CHICORY (AKA BLUE SAILORS)
Chicorium intybus

Introduced

Edible: leaves, flowers, roots

Description

This common perennial is up to 3', with stiff, erect branching stems that are grooved and somewhat hairy. Alternate leaves are similar to dandelion, up to 8" long and 2" across, becoming smaller as they ascend the stem. Lower leaves have a prominent central vein

Chicory basal rosette at optimal collection stage

with hairs along the underside; margins are pinnatifid to sharply dentate, sometimes with broad, deep sinuses. Small, upper leaves are usually lanceolate and sessile, with smooth margins. Leaves bleed milky sap when torn. Blooms May–October, with 2–3 pale- to bright-blue flowers occurring at leaf axils along the stem or at the stem terminus. Each flower is 1"–1½" across, consisting of a corolla with several pale blue stamens and blue anthers at the center and 12–15 narrow radial petals, each with 5 tiny teeth at the tips.

Habitat/Range
Found mostly in open disturbed ground, in fields, pastures, waste areas, abandoned lots, along roadsides and railroads. Native to Europe; range is throughout the United States and Canada.

Uses
Like dandelion, chicory leans to the bitter side in the flavor spectrum, less so when collected early. Young, tender leaves and flowers are good salad ingredients when mixed with milder greens. It is excellent boiled as a potherb, or it can be blanched and seasoned after discarding the water and used in cooked dishes. The root is edible when boiled in a couple of waters, but it is most well known as "Cajun coffee" when roasted and ground as a coffee substitute or additive.

Warnings/Comments
Chicory is commercially cultivated in many countries. Cultivars produce larger, milder leaves and larger roots than their wild counterparts.

TALL WILD LETTUCE (AKA CANADA LETTUCE)
Lactuca canadensis

Native

Edible: leaves

Description
An herbaceous biennial emerging as a basal rosette, with a second-year smooth, green to reddish flower stalk to 8'. Alternate leaves are variable, pale or dark green, occasionally purplish, mostly lanceolate-oblong, with soft hairs on the midrib. Larger leaves are up to 10" long and 3" wide, with deep, pinnate lobes and sparsely-toothed margins. Smaller leaves have shallower lobes or are unlobed. Blooms August–October, with small yellow or pale orange dandelion-like flowers appearing on a narrow panicle at the stem terminus,

Prickly lettuce

each becoming a seed head with a fluff of pappus bristles. The plant exudes a tan or pale orange latex when torn. *L. serriola* (prickly or bitter lettuce) is a similar Eurasian species, but with clasping, pale bluish-green leaves, stiff prickles along the leaf margins and midribs, and a white latex. *L. floridana* (Florida lettuce) has blue flowers and white latex, occasionally with unlobed leaves, and is found in more wooded habitats.

Habitat/Range
Found in glades, thickets, savannas, openings in woodlands, pond and lake borders, riverbanks, glades, fencerows, pastures, old fields, power line cuts, roadsides, vacant lots. Common in disturbed ground, occasionally in pristine habitats. Range is throughout the United States and Canada. Absent from Nevada and Arizona.

Uses
Flavor varies in *Lactuca* species, and in individual plants. Some are quite mild; some are fairly bitter, more so with age. *L. canadensis* seems to be the mildest. Harvest when second-year emerging stalks sprout bunches of early-growth leaves; they are tender

Wild lettuce flower

and mild for salad greens. Older leaves can be boiled as a potherb or mixed with milder greens. Latex of *Lactuca* species is used externally to treat poison ivy rash and other skin irritations. Older sources report mild sedative properties when the latex is dried to make lettuce "opium" (lactucarium); however, no supporting scientific evidence of a sedative compound has been found. It has a history of use in calming syrups and teas, and to treat coughs and upper-respiratory distress.

Warnings/Comments

First cultivated in ancient Egypt, our domestic lettuce varieties are descendants of *L. serriola*. This is another instance where millennia of selective breeding has removed much of the bitterness of the parent native species, along with many of the health benefits. A shining example of this is our ever-present iceberg lettuce, which is mostly water, minimally nutritious, and lacking in vitamins and minerals when compared with its wild counterparts. There are seven *Lactuca* species in the Ozarks.

COMMON SOW THISTLE
Sonchus oleraceus

Introduced

Edible: leaves, flowers, buds

Description

A winter or spring annual up to 3', usually with an erect, solitary stem that
branches only near the terminus when
flowers appear. Alternate leaves are
up to 8" long and 2¼" across, becoming smaller and sparser as they ascend
the central stem. Leaf blades are odd
pinnate with deep triangular lobes;
margins are dentate with soft spines.
The upper leaves can be entire or have
shallow lobes. Yellow ray flowers similar
to dandelions form in tight clusters at
the stem terminus, each flower up to
1¼" across. All parts exude a milky latex
when torn.

Habitat/Range

Prefers open conditions and disturbed
ground, in pastures, fields, roadsides, gardens, yards, vacant lots, near buildings, and waste
areas. Native to Eurasia; range is most of North America and southern Canada.

Uses

Similar to but less bitter than its cousin, dandelion. Sow thistle leaves and flower buds are
a great addition to cooked greens. Cooking softens the prickles and improves the slightly
bitter flavor. Fresh flowers are good in salads. Like all in the dandelion tribe, the young
roots are edible and can be ground and roasted for a coffee stretcher or substitute. (It contains no caffeine, so what's the point?)

Warnings/Comments

An aggressive disturbed-ground colonizer, sow thistle is considered to be an agricultural
pest in some areas.

DANDELION
Taraxacum officinale

Introduced

Edible: leaves, flowers, buds, roots
Primarily known to Americans as a lawn pest, dandelion is possibly the most recognized plant wherever it occurs. Brought here by European settlers as a food source, it is highly prized by foragers as a vitamin-packed salad green, potherb, or coffee substitute.

Description
A low-growing perennial consisting of a basal rosette with oblanceolate, triangular-toothed leaves emerging from a taproot; singly-borne bright yellow ray flowers 1"–1½" across, each on a slender, hollow stem up to 16" tall. The flower matures into a small round seed head embedded with tiny elongated achenes, each with a long slender beak attached to a tuft of parachute-like pappus bristles. This forms the familiar round "blowballs" that enable wind distribution. All parts of the plant exude a white latex when broken.

Habitat/Range

Found in a wide variety of open, disturbed areas, commonly near human habitation. Occurs in lawns, gardens, meadows, vacant lots, roadsides, waste areas, and cropland borders. Native of Eurasia; adventive throughout the United States and Canada.

Uses

Young, tender leaves are great mixed with milder salad greens; can be cooked as a potherb or added to any dish where a slight bitter element is desired. Hold an open flower at the base; pinch and roll between your fingers to push the tasty yellow petals and center out from the bitter green sepals for an attractive salad garnish. Young taproots can be boiled and eaten or can be dried, ground, and roasted for a coffee substitute or additive. Flowers can be fried in batter for fritters or used to make wine after removing the sepals. Used medicinally for a number of ailments. The species name *officinale* was used by Carolus Linnaeus in his 1735 publication *Species Plantarum* to designate established medicinal or culinary use. This publication was the source of the binomial system of nomenclature used in taxonomy today.

Warnings/Comments

Dandelion is a member of a bewilderingly large tribe of similar plants, most of which are edible with similar uses. Many look-alikes are natives, referred to as false dandelions. *Pyrrhopappus carolinianus* (Carolina false dandelion) and *Krigia dandelion* (potato false dandelion) are edible but less common. The latter is named for its tasty round tubers. Due to their aggressive, colonizing nature, millions of dollars are spent annually to eliminate dandelions from lawns and croplands, yet they are grown commercially for culinary and other uses in many countries.

BETULACEAE (BIRCHES, HAZELNUTS)

This family includes 6 genera in about 167 species distributed in temperate and subarctic areas of the Northern Hemisphere, where some reach the northern limit of woody plants. Most are trees and shrubs, several of which are nut-bearing. Also included are alders, hornbeams, hazel-hornbeams, and hop-hornbeams.

AMERICAN HAZELNUT
Corylus americana

Native

Edible: nuts

Description

A thicket-forming medium-size shrub to 12'. Bark is brown to grayish brown, smooth on younger stems, becoming rougher with age. Alternate, simple leaves are 2½"–6" long, oval to ovate, with coarse double-serrate margins and hairy undersides. Male and female flowers form in February–April on the same shrub. Male flowers are yellowish, cylindrical drooping catkins; inconspicuous female flowers form at swollen buds on the stem, with only the red stigmas showing. Nuts form in small green clusters from female flowers, with each ½"–¾" nut surrounded by two papery ragged-edged bracts, ripening to brown in July–early September. Nutshells are brown with a small pale disk at the attachment to the bract; nutmeats are white with brown skin.

Habitat/Range

Found in a variety of soils and conditions, including upland forests and borders, rocky, wooded slopes, fencerows, forested roadway edges, thickets, savannas, and dry prairies. Range is throughout the midwestern and southeastern United States and southern Canada. Absent from Florida and Texas.

Uses

The sweet nutmeats can be shelled and eaten raw, but they taste better after drying and roasting. Use generally as you would other nuts. Chop to use in breads and desserts, make nut milk for flavoring in coffee and sweet dishes, or grind to flour as an ingredient in nut/seedcakes. Straight, unbranched stems are great for making arrow shafts.

Warnings/Comments

C. cornuta (beaked hazelnut) is found in most of the United States and Canada. Absent from the Midwest and a few western states. Larger cultivars are commercially grown and sold as filberts.

BERBERIDACEAE (BARBERRIES, MAYAPPLES)

The family contains about 700 species in 18 genera in varied forms, including spiny-leaved evergreen shrubs, cultivated ground cover, and herbaceous woodland wildflowers such as mayapple. Two species of *Berberis* occur in the Ozarks. *B. canadensis* (Allegheny barberry) is found only rarely in Missouri and has edible berries. *B. thunbergii* (Japanese barberry) is a major invasive pest in some areas.

MAYAPPLE (AKA WILD MANDRAKE)
Podophyllum peltatum

Native

Edible: ripe fruits

If you can beat the critters to them, ripe mayapple fruits are an awesome find, especially when you find a large patch. Some are put off by warnings about the possible toxicity of this plant, but the payoff is a delightful, tropical-flavored treat!

Description

A conspicuous, often colony-forming native perennial with a smooth stalk and large umbrella-shaped leaves, up to 1½' tall. Early leaves appear as a small, furled umbrella emerging from a sheath. Leaves mature to 1' across, each with deep, obovate lobes almost to the central stem and coarse teeth at the outer margins. Infertile plants form singly on a stalk with a terminal peltate leaf. Fertile plants have 2 (occasionally 3) leaves on long petioles forming at the stalk terminus. Blooms late March–May; a single flower up to 3" across develops on a 1" pedicel at the leaf axil, with 6–9 waxy, white petals, a central ovary, and 12–16 yellowish stamens. The flower is replaced by an egg-shaped seed-containing berry up to 2" across, ripening to soft and yellow in late June–July. Only fertile, multiple-leaved plants produce fruit.

Habitat/Range

Found in moist to dry upland deciduous forest, woodland openings, bluff ledges, rich wooded benches near bottomlands, along wooded roadsides and paths. Range is eastern United States and Canada, west to Nebraska and Texas.

Uses

The sweet, tropical-flavored flesh is a great trail nibble and can be used in jams, preserves, desserts, ice cream, and beverages. Harvest fruits only when soft, yellow, and slightly wrinkled—usually when the rest of the plant is dying back. Fruits are difficult to ripen indoors unless already nearly ripe when harvested. When feasible, some suggest covering the plants with old window screens or something similar for protection till fruits ripen fully. Unripe fruits can be toxic; the seeds are mildly so. Consuming a few seeds shouldn't be problematic, but some report a laxative effect, so I usually remove them. Used medicinally to treat a number of ailments.

Warnings/Comments

Only consume ripe fruits. The leaves, root, and unripe fruits contain the toxic compound podophyllotoxin, used in commercial medicines to treat genital warts. It is also being researched for cancer treatment.

BORAGINACEAE (WATERLEAFS, FORGET-ME-NOTS, BORAGES)

This family has a somewhat contentious taxonomic history, but currently contains around 2,700 species in 148 genera; many are native to the western United States. Most species are herbaceous and hairy and can be either annuals or perennials. Some are vines or trees; a few are obligate parasites because they cannot photosynthesize.

VIRGINIA WATERLEAF
Hydrophyllum virginianum

Native

Edible: shoots, leaves, flower buds

Waterleaf is a mild edible with a somewhat sweet flavor when collected early, and is always a great addition to your bag of foraged goodies. It seems to live in the most beautiful places that you'd visit just for the scenery, usually in association with other spring woodland wildflowers near streams and bases of bluffs.

Description

A multistemmed, occasionally colony-forming herbaceous perennial, up to 2' tall. Alternate leaves are on long petioles, up to 6" long and 4" across, pinnately lobed into 3, 5, or 7 leaflets. The opposite lobes are divided by the midrib; margins are coarsely toothed or cleft. Early leaves often have white mottling (appearing as water stains); less so with older, upper leaves. Blooms May–June, first forming as a 2" wide fuzzy cyme on a smooth stalk extending above the leaves, developing into a cluster of 8–20 flowers. Each flower has a bell-shaped corolla up to ½" across, with 5 outer lobes that are pale blue, white, or light pink. Stamens have white, hairlike filaments at the base, with yellow to brown anthers that extend well beyond the corolla.

Waterleaf, young leaf

Habitat/Range

Found in rich deciduous woodlands, wooded ravines and valleys, savannas, bluffs, wooded slopes, and benches along streambanks and woodland paths. Range is throughout the eastern United States and Canada, west to Oklahoma and the Dakotas, south to Arkansas and South Carolina.

Uses

Young, tender shoots, leaves, and unopened flower buds are a great salad addition, good as a potherb, or can be added to soups and other cooked dishes. Medicinally, the raw root was chewed to treat mouth sores or made into tea for diarrhea relief.

Warnings/Comments

The water-stained appearance on early leaves helps separate *H. virginianum* from toxic *Ranunculus* species (buttercups) with similar leaves. If unsure of leaf ID, it's best to harvest plants that are in or nearing bloom. Other less-common *Hydrophyllum* species include *H. appendiculatum* (great waterleaf) and *H. canadense* (blunt-leaved waterleaf); both have leaves that are palmately 5-lobed, similar to maple leaves.

VIRGINIA BLUEBELLS
(AKA COWSLIP, LUNGWORT OYSTERLEAF)
Mertensia virginica

Native

Edible: shoots, leaves, flowers

Description

A showy early-spring perennial to 2' tall with large, smooth fleshy leaves and clusters of pale-blue flowers. The central stem is pale green and smooth, with large alternate leaves at the base; the leaves become smaller as they ascend the stem. Lower leaves are bluish green, up to 6" long, tapering into winged petioles at the base. They are broadly ovate, with smooth margins and a soft and floppy appearance; stem leaves are elliptical, smaller, and mostly sessile. Clusters of pink buds form on cymes at the stem terminus, eventually maturing to clusters of nodding flowers. Individual flowers are up to 1¼" in length, with a bell-shaped outer corolla that narrows to a tubular base at its calyx. Most flowers are pale to medium blue, with variants that are occasionally pink, rarely white. This may be one of the only species in Boraginaceae that isn't hairy.

Habitat/Range
Found primarily in rich soil conditions, in swamps, wooded floodplains, bottomland forests, bottoms of wooded ravines, bases and ledges of bluffs, and banks of streams and rivers. It can form large colonies, where it competes with *Laportea canadensis* (wood nettle). Range is midwestern and eastern United States and Canada, west to eastern Kansas and Nebraska. Absent from Louisiana, Florida, and South Carolina.

Uses
Leaves, young tender flower stems, and flowers have a somewhat succulent texture and mild flavor, making them a good salad addition. They can also be used as a lightly cooked potherb. The common name oysterleaf is from accounts of their flavor being faintly reminiscent of oysters. The common name lungwort refers to medicinal use in treatment of lung, bronchial, or other respiratory ailments, and it is used medicinally like other species in the family Boraginaceae, such as comfrey (*Cynoglossum officinale*). "Cowslip" is a reference to this and other unrelated plants found in meadows grazed by cows. In particular, it refers to something cows leave behind that one might slip on.

Warnings/Comments
Observe the usual cautions when collecting natives. Some older sources report the plant as inedible, but I've yet to find any reference to toxic constituents. Due to its popularity as a garden ornamental and ease of transplanting, this plant has become a target for unethical collectors, who sometimes remove entire populations from the wild, leaving only craters under the trees. If buying plants from nurseries, make sure they were propagated from seed and not collected from the wild.

BRASSICACEAE (MUSTARDS)

This economically important family contains 4,060 species in 372 genera. The European species *Brassica oleracea* was selectively bred or altered over time to produce six of the most popular vegetables in the family. Each alteration produced a different vegetable by developing a different plant part, as follows: cabbage—terminal leaf bud; brussels sprouts—lateral leaf buds; kale—leaves; kohlrabi—stem; broccoli—stem and flower buds; cauliflower—flower buds. The family also includes other cruciferous vegetables, such as collards, radishes, turnips, and rutabagas. All forms have characteristic four-petaled flowers.

GARLIC MUSTARD
Alliaria petiolate

Introduced

Edible: shoots, leaves, flowers

Description

A biennial, weak-stemmed herb up to 3' tall, with one to many flowering stems from each root. First-year basal rosette leaves are up to 2" across, on long, slender petioles. They are generally orbicular with a prominent network of veins and have wavy or scalloped margins. Alternate flower-stem leaves are on short petioles and are generally triangular, with sharply toothed margins. Numerous small white flowers appear at terminal racemes and at the leaf axil. Flowers mature to siliques up to 3" long.

Habitat/Range

Highly invasive. Occurs in forested bottoms, open woodlands, gardens, along streams and woodland paths, and in partly shaded conditions in fertile, loamy soil or disturbed ground. Native to Eurasia, it was introduced into the United States in the 1970s and is spreading rapidly. It is undoubtedly more widespread than current records indicate.

Uses

All aboveground parts have the pungent flavor typical of mustards, with a nice garlic undertone. Tender leaves are best raw before flowering, and can be added to salads or used as an ingredient in soups, sauces, and flavorings. The leaves also make a good pot-herb, a delicious pesto, or can be chopped fine and mixed with salt to make a tasty bouil-lon for soups. The seeds can be ground to make a hot mustard.

Warnings/Comments

This plant grows rapidly and abundantly, and will shade out or outcompete natives in many habitats. As with all harmful and aggressive invasives, harvest carefully to avoid introducing seeds into new areas. The upshot is that it's a tasty edible that can be harvested without limits. The best scenario, however unlikely, would be to eat it into oblivion.

RECIPE

Garlic Mustard Bouillon

4 ounces sea salt

16 ounces (roughly 4 cups) garlic mustard greens. (Other seasonal tasty greens and seasonings may be used; mix and match for great flavor combinations.)

Note: A kitchen scale is helpful to get the correct measurement; it should be a 4-to-1 weight ratio of greens to salt (1 cup chopped greens is equal to about 4 ounces).

Mince greens and mix in a bowl with the salt, or add both to a food processor and pulse till greens are finely chopped. Put mixture into glass jars with plastic lids (salt will corrode metal).

The bouillon will store for up to a year; it can be used to flavor soups and other dishes, as a meat rub or a brine, in hummus and pesto, or mixed into sour cream for a colorful and flavorful dip or dish topping.

Wintercress in bloom, with seeds

WINTERCRESS (AKA YELLOW ROCKET)
Barbarea vulgaris

Introduced

Edible: shoots, leaves, flowers

Description
A leafy, branched biennial up to 2" tall. The first-year basal rosette is up to 1' across; 1 or more flowering stalks appear the second year. Basal leaves are on long petioles, with opposite lateral lobes and a larger, ovate terminal lobe. Blade surface is shiny dark green;

margins are undulate to shallowly lobed. Alternate leaves on the flower stalk are bluntly toothed, becoming smaller and sessile as they ascend the stem. Blooms April–June, forming bunches of small yellow, 4-petaled flowers at each stem terminus. Flowers mature to produce slender, cylindrical seeds called siliques.

Habitat/Range
Found in cultivated or fallow fields, pastures, gardens, vacant lots, and along roadsides, streams, and railroads. Prefers open, disturbed areas. Native to Eurasia; naturalized over most of North America not long after European colonization.

Uses
Young basal rosette leaves are a dandy boiled green, and can be found nearly

Wintercress flower buds

any time of the year. Young shoots and the tender ends of second-year stems are also good when the flower buds are still tight but get bitter as they mature. Occasionally young flower buds are mild enough to eat raw, but not often. A bit of boiling is the key; steaming and other cooking methods do not always remove the bitterness.

Warnings/Comments
Recent studies have concluded that consuming large amounts can interfere with kidney function.

Wintercress basal rosette

SHEPHERD'S PURSE
Capsella bursa-pastoris

Introduced

Edible: all parts

Description
A summer or winter annual that forms a basal rosette and a single or sparsely-branched flower stalk up to 2'. Basal leaves are lanceolate or oblanceolate, with deep pinnate lobes, up to 4½" long and ¾" wide. The main flower stalk and lower branches terminate in a raceme of tiny 4-petaled flowers, with a small, clasping lanceolate leaf at each branch axil. Each flower is less than ⅛" across, maturing into a 2-lobed triangular or heart-shaped flattened seedpod on a slender, ascending pedicel. The flowering racemes elongate with age.

Habitat/Range
Found in nearly any disturbed, open habitat. Occurs in lawns, gardens, vacant lots, roadsides, pastures, and fields. A native of Europe, it ranges throughout the United States and Canada and is one of the most widespread plants on the planet due to anthropogenic distribution.

Uses
Young pre-flowering basal leaves, tender stem tops, flowers, and seedpods are a great salad addition with a broccoli-like flavor. Older leaves become peppery but can be boiled as a potherb or used in cooked dishes. The root can be boiled as a vegetable or dried and ground for a ginger substitute. Widely used as a medicinal for numerous ailments.

Warnings/Comments
As with many plants, consumption of large quantities isn't advised. Reported symptoms from overconsumption are drowsiness, changes in blood pressure or thyroid function, heart palpitations, and miscarriages during pregnancy, although I suspect one would have to eat a bellyful to experience those symptoms.

CUT-LEAVED TOOTHWORT
Cardamine concatinata

Native

Edible: all parts

It's always a spectacular sight to see this early-spring ephemeral in carpets of blooms with spring beauty, trout lily, rue anemone, Virginia waterleaf, and others. And it provides a nice snack!

Description

A native herbaceous perennial up to 10" tall, with single basal leaves on petioles or a single, erect flowering stem with 3 cauline leaves in a whorl around the midpoint. Leaves are up to 3" long and across, deeply dissected into 3–5 narrow palmate lobes, each with toothed margins. Blooms March–May; the flowering stem terminates in a floppy panicle of several white or pale pink 4-petaled flowers, each up to ½" across. Flowers mature to slender, elongated seeds typical of Brassicaceae. The roots are shallow, elongated tubers with toothlike projections, often growing horizontal to the stem.

Habitat/Range

Found in rich, wooded habitats, moist ravines and slopes, bottomland forests, and wooded benches along streams. Range is throughout eastern and midwestern United States and Canada, west to Texas and the Dakotas.

Cut-leaved toothwort root

Uses

Raw young leaves and upper stems, flowers, and tubers are a nice pungent trail nibble or salad addition, or can be added to soups or other cooked dishes. Young tubers have a crisp texture and peppery horseradish-like flavor that can get strong with age; older tubers can be dried and ground as a horseradish substitute.

Warnings/Comments

As with all natives, limit collection to preserve the ability to reproduce, and only dig roots when found in colonies. The genus is represented by about 150 species worldwide.

HAIRY BITTERCRESS
Cardamine hirsute

Introduced

Edible: leaves, stems, seeds, roots

Description
A weak-stemmed biannual or winter
annual, initially emerging from a basal
rosette. Flowering stem is up to 10"
tall, with sparse, fine hairs at its base,
often becoming smooth in its upper
parts. Basal leaves are up to 4" long,
odd-pinnately compound, with 5–9
orbicular to ovate leaflets, with a larger
terminal leaflet. Flowering stem leaflets
are linear to oblanceolate, smaller and
fewer than basal leaflets. Flowers are
small and white, maturing to 1" long,
slender siliques typical of mustards.

Habitat/Range
Prefers moist soil conditions in disturbed ground and open habitats. Occurs in lawns,
borders of croplands and nurseries, old fields, waste areas, and along woodland paths and
roadsides. Commonly found in the eastern United States and Canada, US–Mexican border
states, and western coastal states. Absent from much of the upper Midwest and central-
western states.

Uses
Despite the name, most of the bittercress species I've tasted have a pleasant, peppery flavor similar to watercress. Use the tender tops to spice up mild salads or potherb greens, or
use raw or cooked in other dishes to add flavor. Like other mustards, the seeds and roots
can be crushed then mixed with vinegar, salt, and other seasoning to make a mustard
condiment.

Warnings/Comments
C. bulbosa (spring cress), *C. parviflora* (small-flowered bittercress), and *C. pennsylvanica*
(Pennsylvania bittercress) are natives and are three of the seven members of the genus
found in the Ozarks. Most are fine raw for salads. Others may be too bitter or peppery and
are best used as potherbs or condiments.

PEPPERGRASS (AKA FIELD CRESS, POOR MAN'S PEPPER)
Lepidium spp.

Both Native and Introduced

Edible: basal leaves, tender tops, roots

Description
Low-growing basal rosette leaves are up to 3" long and have pinnate lobes similar to dandelion. The flowering stem is up to 15" tall, with alternate stem leaves that are ovate to slender, with entire to toothed margins. The upper stem branches into cylindrical, flowering racemes up to 4" long (like a small bottlebrush) and have the small 4-petaled flowers typical of mustards. Flowers mature to flattened, oval to round seeds, often with a small cleft at the tip.

Habitat/Range
Occurs in open, disturbed ground, fields, pastures, roadsides, lawns, gardens, and vacant lots. Several similar *Lepidium* species are found in the Ozarks; the most common are the Eurasian species *L. campestre*, and the US native *L. virginicum*.

Uses
The seeds really do taste like black pepper and can be used to flavor meats, soups, and other cooked dishes. Tender tops with leaves and flowers can be added raw to salads and are especially tasty when paired with wood or field sorrel leaves for a lemon-pepper flavoring. The seeds can be dried and ground for a pepper substitute. The young root can be eaten raw as a somewhat pungent trail nibble or ground and mixed with vinegar for a horseradish substitute.

Warnings/Comments
A few allergic reactions have been reported; sample cautiously before consuming any quantity. Around 170 *Lepidium* species occur globally, with approximately 56 in North America. The plant was cultivated by indigenous peoples.

WATERCRESS
Rorippa nasturtium-aquaticum (previously *Nasturtium officinale*)

Introduced

Edible: upper leaves

Watercress was my mom's favorite wild salad green; we gathered it at the nearby Okino Dairy Farm, where it still grows abundantly near the springhouse milk cooler at the spring source of Pearson Creek. The water was surely contaminated with *E. coli* from the large pasture atop the hill and occasional cows that got into the spring, but we never had problems. Maybe the watercress was decontaminated by the hot bacon grease and vinegar she always put on it—or possibly because our 50-foot-deep well never passed a water test and we were just used to it.

Description

This low-growing aquatic perennial often forms large mats in shallow springs, seeps, and along cold-water streambanks. Long rootlets along the stem at leaf nodes allow it to root into mud or gravel bottoms, where it forms dense colonies that can often grow to a height of 1' above the water's surface. Alternate leaves are clasping, bipinnately compound, 3"–6" long, with 3–9 leaflets, usually with a rounded leaflet at the top and several opposite, rounded leaflets along the leaf axil. White flowers appear in April, forming in clusters on short-stemmed racemes at the tips of stems; each is 4-petaled and around ¼" across. Seedpods are long and thin, typical of Brassicaceae.

Habitat/Range

Found in flowing, cold water of springs and spring branches, seeps, fens, spring-fed marshes, and streambanks. Occasionally roots in soil. Originally native to Eurasia; occurs throughout North America. Widely distributed globally due to cultivation.

Uses

A very nutritious and popular salad green known for its pungent, peppery flavor and numerous health benefits. Can be used as a steamed vegetable or added to soups or other cooked dishes to spice up the flavor. Best harvested before flowering; afterward it can get "bitey." Seeds can be sprouted; shoots can be harvested days after germination. Used medicinally for a number of ailments.

Warnings/Comments

Always collect from a few inches above the waterline to avoid parasites like liver flukes and *giardia*; wash well to avoid possible *E. coli* contamination. If you're unsure of the water quality, always cook watercress to pasteurization temperature. Studies have identified more than 15 essential vitamins and minerals in watercress, more iron than spinach, more calcium than milk, and more vitamin C than oranges. It is grown hydroponically and cultivated around the world, becoming increasingly available at supermarkets. Its former name *Nasturtium* is Latin for "nose twister," named for its peppery flavor.

RECIPE

Watercress Soft Tacos

Fresh, early watercress tops, washed or lightly blanched

Corn tortillas

Hummus

Salsa picante

Dry Mexican cheese

Lightly toast the tortillas in a skillet. Add a very light smear of hummus, pesto, or mayo to each tortilla. Lay on a small bunch of watercress; top with salsa picante or pico de gallo, and a bit of crumbled Mexican or other dry cheese.

CACTACEAE (CACTI)

This is a mostly new-world family consisting of 1,866 species in 131 genera. Most cacti are adapted to arid environments, although several species are native to rain forests and other tropical or subtropical areas. Many have succulent photosynthetic stems, reduced leaves that are often modified as spines, and showy, numerous-petaled flowers.

EASTERN PRICKLY PEAR
Opuntia humifisa

Native

Edible: young pads, fruits, seeds

Many are surprised to see prickly pear cactus in the forested eastern United States. Our small native can be used similarly to the large western species and thornless cultivars popular in Mexican cuisine. Nopals (pads) and tunas (fruits) are occasionally found in supermarkets.

Description

A low-growing cactus with succulent, ovoid or paddle-shaped pads up to 7" long and 5" wide, each dotted with areoles (air pores) in sparse rows. Each areole contains a tuft of brown, woolly hairs with tiny, sharp bristles (glochids) and typically has one to several longer, stiff spines. Blooms May–July, with one to several buds forming at the top of mature pads. Showy yellow flowers are up to 3" across, each with numerous central stamens and many tepals; the innermost tepals often show an orange blotch. In late summer, flowers are replaced by pear-shaped purplish fruits up to 1½" long, each with a concave depression at the top and sparse tufts of glochidia on the outer surface. Fruits contain several roundish seeds surrounded by greenish or purplish sweet flesh.

Habitat/Range

Prefers dry, open habitats. Found on glades, bluff tops and ledges, dry benches along rivers, near exposed bedrock in upland or sand prairies, rocky pastures, along roadsides and railroads. Range is mostly eastern and midwestern United States, west to New Mexico and Montana. Absent from Wyoming, North Dakota, and upper New England.

Uses

Very young pads can be eaten raw or cooked after removing glochidia, best harvested before spines develop. Older pads can be peeled and the tough edges trimmed off; the flesh is somewhat mucilaginous. Harvest with thick gloves or tongs; remove spines and glochidia by burning off by flame or by rubbing in sand and rinsing thoroughly. Pads are good flame-roasted, sliced thin, and used like string beans, fried like onion rings, or used in any cooked dish when a thickener is desired. The tunas have a sweet-tart flesh that is good raw as a trail nibble or can be collected for use in jams, jellies, syrups, sauces, and wines and other beverages. The hard seeds should be removed, or they can be roasted and ground for use as a flour additive. The gel-like juice from pads is used to treat and soothe burns and skin conditions; its uses are similar to aloe vera.

Prickly pear tunas

Warnings/Comments

Be thorough in cleaning both pads and fruits; missed glochids are not fun when embedded in your tongue.

RECIPE

Grilled Prickly Pear Tacos

Corn or flour tortillas

Filling:

6 or so young, thoroughly cleaned prickly pear pads

1 small onion, sliced into ½"-thick rounds

1–2 jalapeños, sliced in half and seeds removed

1 teaspoon cumin

Dash of garlic powder

Salt to taste

1 can (16 ounces) black beans or 2 cups wild beans

1 tablespoon olive oil

Topping:

2 cups finely-sliced red cabbage and/or zesty wild greens

1 tablespoon lime juice

½ cup chopped cilantro

½ cup cotija or other dry cheese

1. In a small pan, heat beans. Add cumin and garlic powder; salt to taste and set aside.

2. Add lime juice and cilantro to sliced cabbage or greens; salt to taste and set aside.

3. Drizzle pads, onion, and jalapeños with olive oil; grill until slightly charred. Salt to taste, and slice all into taco-friendly strips.

4. Heat or slightly grill tortillas. Place a line of filling, black beans, cabbage topping, and cheese in the center.

5. Serve with roasted tomato–ground cherry salsa and chips. Pair with a sumac lemonade margarita flavored with prickly pear fruit syrup.

CANNABACEAE (CANNABIS, HACKBERRIES, HOPS)

This family has about 170 species grouped into 11 genera and can appear as trees, vines, or herbs. One of these herbs has recently become a powerful but controversial economic driver in some states.

COMMON HACKBERRY
Celtis occidentalis

Native

Edible: fruits

Hackberry fruits could be described as a nut/fruit hybrid; they have a thin skin of sweet flesh covering a hard-shelled seed that has an oily and nut-like center. They also persist on the tree into winter, providing cold-season foraging opportunities.

Description

A straight-trunked tree with a rounded crown, up to 80' tall. The bark is mostly smooth and gray when young, developing distinctive warty projections and corky ridges with age. Alternate leaves are broadly to narrowly ovate, with an asymmetrical base, serrated margins, and a pointed tip. Flowers April–May, with male, female, and perfect flowers on the same tree. Flowers are yellow-green, ¼" across. In September–October female flowers mature into round, purplish-black to orange drupes up to ½" across. Each drupe contains a seed with a round, hard shell surrounded by a thin layer of somewhat-dry flesh.

Habitat/Range

Found in bottomlands, moist upland slopes, savannas, fencerows, and riverbanks. Prefers rich soil, but will grow in many soil conditions. Range is west to North Dakota and northern Oklahoma, south to northern Arkansas and Tennessee, east to Massachusetts and North Carolina.

Uses

The berry flesh makes a nice trail nibble. The seed interior is also edible and nutritious, but the woody covering is often hard enough to break a tooth. (See recipe below for processing tips.) To make a sweet beverage, break the skins up a bit. Put the berries into a jar and cover with hot water to soak. Agitate and stir frequently till the flesh softens and dissolves in the water; pour through a strainer to remove seeds and skins.

Ridged hackberry bark

The exposed, oily meat inside the hackberry seed

Warnings/Comments

As mentioned above, biting the seeds can break teeth. There are two other *Celtis* species in the Ozarks. *C. laevigata* (sugarberry) has narrower leaves and larger fruits, a more southern range, and prefers bottomlands. *C. tenuifolia* (dwarf hackberry) is generally shorter and shrub-like, with smaller fruits. It is found mostly in glades and dry, open habitats.

RECIPE

Hackberry Candy Bars

4 -5 cups hackberries

1 tablespoon honey or maple syrup

½ cup hickory nuts or hazelnuts, crushed

½ cup dried fruit or berries, finely chopped

Use a mortar and pestle or *molcajete* to thoroughly pulverize the whole fruits. The fruit flesh and oily meat inside the seeds will give the mush a stiff cookie dough–like texture, and it's quite tasty at this stage. To make no-cook candy bars, combine ingredients; mix well. Roll out mixture thin between layers of waxed paper or plastic wrap.

Note: The mixture will contain tiny seed-hull fragments that are easily avoided by not biting down too hard while chewing. To avoid the woody bits entirely, put the crushed fruits in a pan with a bit of water and simmer while stirring to loosen up the flesh and soften the seeds. Pour through a fine strainer or cheesecloth to remove the hull remnants.

Hackberry Candy Bars

CAPRIFOLIACEAE (CORN SALADS, HONEYSUCKLES)

This cosmopolitan family consists of around 860 species in 42 genera. A few species are herbaceous, but most are woody vines or shrubs, many of which are grown ornamentally. Some have escaped cultivation to become invasive pests, such as *Lonicera japonica* (Japanese honeysuckle) and *L. mackii* (bush or Amur honeysuckle).

CORN SALAD (AKA BEAKED CORN SALAD)
Valerianella radiata

Native

Edible: leaves, stems, flowers

Description

A low annual with a 4-sided, doubly-branching stem up to 1' tall, emerging from a basal rosette. Opposite leaves are up to 3" long and 1" wide, sessile and clasping, oblong or oblanceolate, with smooth or coarsely-toothed margins. Flat-topped clusters of white flowers emerge at the stem terminus; each is ⅛" across and 5-lobed, often forming in parallel or rectangular rows.

Habitat/Range

Found in moist prairies, glades, rocky slopes, open stream bottoms and valleys, fallow croplands, waste areas, and along railroads and roadsides. Range is throughout the southern two-thirds of the United States, east to New York and Florida, west to Kansas and Texas.

Uses

Use as lettuce. As the name implies, the young leaves, flowers, and upper stems are great mild-flavored salad greens. Leaves are best when picked before the flowers appear, April–May.

Warnings/Comments

The Ozarks are home to several *Valerianella* species. *V. locusta* (lamb's lettuce, or mâche) is a Eurasian adventive; the name corn salad comes from its popularity there as a wild salad green found at the edges of cornfields. *V. ozarkana* (previously *V. bushii*, Ozark corn salad) is a rare endemic found only in parts of southern Missouri, Arkansas, and Oklahoma, referred to in older references as "Benjamin Franklin bush." Oddly enough, Benjamin Franklin Bush was a botanist/ornithologist whose life's work was to catalog the flora of Jackson County, Missouri. In this work, published in 1882, he described several previously unknown local plants; several species were named *bushii* in his honor.

CARYOPHYLLACEAE (CHICKWEEDS, CARNATIONS, PINKS)

This large, mostly herbaceous family has 2,625 known species in 81 genera. Many are cultivated as ornamental garden flowers; a few species, such as common chickweed, are considered to be pests and weeds.

COMMON CHICKWEED
Stellaria media

Introduced

Edible: leaves, stems

When you are craving fresh, nutritious wild greens in midwinter, look for clumps of chickweed and several other edibles around protected areas near springs, bases of slopes, or piles of leaf litter. It will pop up nearly any time of the year when there is adequate moisture and several days of above-freezing temps.

Description

A low-growing, annual/perennial with branching stems up to 1' long. Weak colony-forming stems are prostrate from the base, becoming erect at the upper portion, rooting at the nodes. Color is light green to occasionally burgundy, with a single, linear row of

Common chickweed with flower PHOTO BY DEBORAH TYLER

small hairs. Pairs of opposite leaves occur along stems; leaves are ovate to deltoid, up to 1" long and ¾" wide, but usually smaller. Leaves have petioles on lower pairs, are sessile on upper pairs. Small flowers occur at leaf axils and on cymes at the branch tips, each ¼" across with a pale green central ovary; the 5 white petals are so deeply cleft as to appear as 10 petals.

Habitat/Range
Occurs in mostly moist soil or disturbed ground in lawns, gardens, cropland, in bottom-lands, near springs, ponds and rich soil near streambanks, damp meadows, and waste areas. Native to Eurasia; found throughout the United States and Canada. Found almost globally due to anthropogenic distribution.

Uses
Young, tender tops and leaves are good raw, as a mild salad green; chop up older stems to avoid the stringiness. They can be steamed or lightly boiled or used as a spinach substitute in pesto, breads, quiche, soups, and other cooked dishes. When adding to soups, add during the last few minutes as to not overcook.

Warnings/Comments
Chickweeds have fairly high levels of saponins and can cause gastric distress in some when eaten in large quantity. *Cerastium fontanum* (mouse-ear chickweed) is similar, with rounded, hairy leaves. It is also edible, but better if cooked.

EBENACEAE (PERSIMMONS, EBONIES)

This family of mostly trees and shrubs contains around 500 species in 4 genera. Several species are known for their beautiful wood; a few are cultivated for their fruits.

AMERICAN PERSIMMON
Diospyros virginiana

Native

Edible: fruits

Many kids in the rural Ozarks grew up gathering persimmons so our moms would make bread or pudding for dessert. When unknowing friends or relatives would come to visit in the fall (being the ornery brats we were), we'd find a tree with a few ripe fruits and eat one, say how sweet it was, then hand them an unripe fruit to watch the fun! The astringent paste of unripe fruit sticks to the tongue with a high amount of pucker power, and I learned quickly not to do this to kids who were bigger or faster than I was.

Description

Persimmon trees can grow to 65' but are usually smaller, often fruiting at 10'. Simple alternate leaves are glossy and leathery with smooth margins, 2"–6" long, 1"–3" wide. Distinctive bark is dark colored and deeply grooved, with ridges broken into rectangular blocks. Small, fragrant, urn-shaped flowers appear in midsummer, each with 4 decurved white lobes. Smaller male flowers appear in clusters; solitary female flowers up to ⅔" across mature to produce globe-shaped green fruits ¾"–1½" across, each containing up to 6 flattened-oval seeds. Ripening begins in late September, when fruits turn orange with purplish hues. When fully ripe, they are soft and slightly wrinkled, and the skin has a translucent appearance. Many will not fully ripen to full sweetness until after a hard frost in October or November.

Persimmon ground fall

Habitat/Range
Found in open dry woods, bottomlands, glades, prairies, old fields, stream/forest edges, fencerows, and thickets. Distributed throughout the southeastern United States, south to the Gulf Coast, north to the southern third of Missouri and southern Illinois, east to the Atlantic coast and southern portions of some mid-Atlantic states, west to eastern Texas and southeast Kansas.

Uses
The sweet, ripe fruits are great on the spot. To process, press the fruits through a metal colander or chinois to remove the seeds and skins. Use the pulp in desserts, puddings, breads, sweet soups, and other dishes, or freeze for later. Spread a thin layer of pulp on wax paper or plastic wrap and dry to make fruit leather, or dry the fruits whole. Brandied persimmons are a great cordial, or use them to make beer, if that is your thing. The dried leaves make a great tea that is packed full of antioxidants, and contains antiviral, anticarcinogenic and other beneficial compounds. The dark heartwood has been used to make golf clubs, and is highly regarded as a superior bow wood. It has similar valuable properties to its tropical relative, ebony.

Warnings/Comments
According to folklore, splitting the seeds can predict the severity of the winter. Inside the seed halves, the 2 cotyledon leaves will appear as one of three different shapes. When perfectly superimposed and appearing as a spoon, expect heavy snow. If underdeveloped and appearing as a knife, it will be cold and windy. If the shape is slightly offset and resembles a fork, expect a mild winter. According to scientific studies, the shapes more likely reflect the severity of the previous winter. *Diospyros kaki* (Japanese persimmon) is an Asian cultivar that is sold commercially.

Persimmon Mousse with Spicebush/Wild Ginger Crumble

Crumble:

½ cup white flour

1 tablespoon butter

1 teaspoon powdered sugar

1 teaspoon dried, powdered spicebush berries and/or wild ginger root (or substitute ½ teaspoon cardamom, ginger, or allspice)

Mousse:

3 cups persimmon pulp

2 cups whipped cream

Dash of lemon juice

¼ teaspoon vanilla

Optional: If more sweetness is desired, add ¼ cup powdered sugar or a bit of stevia.

1. Mix crumble ingredients to a rough breadcrumb texture. Scatter on a flat pan and bake at low heat until lightly browned.

2. Gently mix mousse ingredients together until fluffy and smooth. **Note:** Pawpaw can be substituted for persimmon; blueberries or other berries are a nice addition.

3. Serve mousse in pudding cups; top with crumble.

Mousse made with pawpaws and blueberries

ELAEAGNACEAE (SILVERBERRIES, OLEASTERS)

This small family has about 60 species in 3 genera; most have stems with thorns and simple leaves with scales or hairs. Several species are horticulturally important, and several are cultivated for the edible berries; a few, such as Russian olive, have become invasive pests. The United States has 3 native species in the genus *Shepherdia* (buffaloberry) that have similar characteristics and edible, if somewhat bitter, berries. All have more western or northern ranges and do not occur in the Ozarks.

AUTUMN OLIVE
(AKA JAPANESE SILVERBERRY, AUTUMNBERRY)
Elaeagnus umbellata

Introduced

Edible: fruits

Description

An invasive shrub to 20', usually with spreading multiple stems. Bark on smaller stems is grayish brown and smooth, often with lenticels and short thorns. Trunk bark (if present) is gray and furrowed. Young twigs are silvery to green with small scales. Alternate leaves are up to 3" long and 1¼" across, elliptic-oblong to ovate with smooth wavy margins. Upper leaf surface is light green with sparse scales; undersides are pale green to whitish with dense silvery scales. In April–May, fragrant flowers form along stems at the leaf axil in small umbel-like clusters. Each flower is a ½" long tubular calyx with 4 lobes that appear as petals. Each plant can produce a prodigious number of drupe-like fleshy ⅓" fruits that are pink to red at maturity and finely dotted with silver scales.

Habitat/Range
This Asian species was originally planted as an ornamental to prevent erosion along roadways and in wildlife areas to provide food and cover. It naturalized to become an aggressive, drought-resistant invasive that tolerates poor soils. Found along fencerows, roadway/power line cuts, thickets, fields, pastures, grasslands, sparse woodlands, and borders. Range is mostly eastern North America and Ontario, west to Kansas and Nebraska. Also naturalized in Montana, Washington, and Oregon.

Uses
The astringent, sweet-tart ripe fruits are great raw as a trail nibble but are highly variable in flavor. Make syrup by cooking the fruits in a bit of water. Mash (or use a food processor) to liquefy the flesh; strain out the seeds. Use the syrup to make excellent sauces, cocktails, fruit leather, or jam or jelly. Jelly made with autumn olive will often have different consistencies that will separate in the jar, giving it a swirled appearance. Used medicinally for a number of ailments, especially pulmonary infections. Ongoing studies indicate immune-building and cancer-fighting properties.

Warnings/Comments
Avoid spreading viable seeds due to the plant's invasive nature; the cooking process of making syrup will kill the live germ. The silvery-white leaf undersides and small dots on the fruits separate *E. umbellata* from other shrubs with red berries. The berries contain up to 18 times the antioxidant lycopene than tomatoes and are high in other antioxidants and vitamin C.

ERICACEAE (BLUEBERRIES, HEATHS)

This large family consists of about 4,250 known species across 124 genera and occurs nearly worldwide. Many members have flowers that are often urn-shaped with fused petals, though some species have unfused bilaterally symmetrical flowers; fruits are usually a berry or capsule. Many can tolerate poor acidic soils. The family includes many economically important species, including cranberries, blueberries, and rhododendrons.

MIKOLA249, ISTOCK

WILD BLUEBERRIES: HILLSIDE BLUEBERRY, DEERBERRY, TREE FARKLEBERRY
Vaccinium pallidum, V. stamineum, V. arboretum

Native

Edible: berries

During 35 years as a wildlife field biologist, I've had the good fortune to work in many wild places around the country. A good perk of the job is running across a ripe blueberry patch—unless a bear wants that patch!

Description

Vacciniums are colony-forming, woody-stemmed branching shrubs with alternate simple leaves. Their dark purple berries often have a star-shaped appendage at the bottom. *V. pallidum* (hillside blueberry) is usually 1'–2' tall, with multiple stems. Young stems are green or yellowish green, maturing to reddish or yellowish brown, with shredding bark on older specimens. Leaves are ¾"–2¼" long, ½"–1" across, ovate, obovate, or broadly elliptic, with smooth margins. Blooms in late spring, with drooping flowers forming in clusters at terminal ends of second-year branches. Each flower has a white to pink urn-shaped tubular corolla with 5 tiny, recurved lobes, maturing to a ¼" globoid fruit that ripens dark blue to purple-black. *V. stamineum* (deerberry) is generally larger, with bell-shaped white flowers, larger leaves with pale undersides and pointed tips, and larger berries; both ripen in late June. *V. arboretum* (tree farkle-berry) grows as a single-trunked, many-branched small tree up to 6'–25'. Older specimens have red, gray, or brown shred-ding bark. Leaves are shiny and leathery. Blooms later than other *Vacciniums*, with small, dry fruits appearing in late fall.

Deerberry

Farkleberry

Habitat/Range
All *Vaccinium* species prefer acidic soil and can be found in both oak-hickory and short-leaf pine habitats. Found in dry, open upland forest, rocky slopes, glades, savannas, rocky ledges, tops and margins of bluffs, and sandy ridges. Range of all 3 species is generally eastern and midwestern United States. *V. arboretum* has a more southern range and is found south of Illinois and Indiana.

Uses
Use like any berry; all are high in vitamin C and antioxidants. Great raw as a trail nibble or dessert topping. Excellent for use in jams, sauces, wines, cordials, smoothies; can be frozen or dried for later use. Berries of *V. pallidum* are the sweetest and are perfect in pancakes, breads, and other confections. *V. stamineum* berries are generally tart and a good choice for pies, cobblers, and sauces. *V. arboretum* berries are the least flavorful but are a good late-season find when other berries are long gone.

Warnings/Comments
Vaccinium is a widespread genus, from 3"-tall varieties found in alpine tundra to the 25'-tall *V. arboretum*. Many large-berried cultivars are grown and sold commercially.

FABACEAE (BEANS, PEAS, LEGUMES)

This large and economically important family harbors about 19,000 known species in 751 genera, and is second only to Poaceae (grasses) in its agricultural significance and percentage of human diet. It is third in number of species after Orchidaceae and Asteraceae, and contains trees, shrubs, vines, and perennial or annual herbaceous plants, many of which are easily recognized by their characteristic pea flowers, legume fruits and compound leaves.

Hog peanut flowers, with pods

HOG PEANUT, TRAILING FUZZY BEAN
Amphicarpaea bracteata, Strophostyles helvula

Native

Edible: beans, roots, ground fruits

Description

Hog peanut is a trailing or climbing, often aggressive vine up to 8', with alternate, trifoliate leaves occurring at intervals along the stem. Leaflets are broadly lanceolate to ovate, with smooth margins. The terminal leaflet is up to 2½" long, on a petiole, and is larger than the mostly-sessile lateral leaflets. Flower stalks form at intervals on the stem at leaf axils, with up to 12 flowers emerging on compact racemes up to 2" long. Flowers are ½" long, pale pink to lavender, each having 2 upright petals rolled at the edges, 2 slender lateral lobes, and a small keel. Flowers mature to flattened, curved pods up to 1½" long, each containing 3 or 4 mottled grayish beans. In addition, it produces inconspicuous secondary flowers

Trailing fuzzy bean

that mature to a ½" or larger round or pear-shaped fruit (peanut) from the root stolons, at or below the ground. *Strophostyles helvula* (trailing fuzzy bean) has larger, similar leaves that are rarely lobed, and lacks the ground fruits. Individual flowers only bloom a few at a time and consist of an upright, flaring pink petal, 2 slender lateral petals, and a pronounced upright-curved keel. Flowers mature to clusters of cylindrical, fuzzy pods up to 3½" long, each containing several black, shiny beans.

Hog peanut beans

Habitat/Range

A. bracteata is found in generally moist, rich soil conditions, in open to shaded bottoms and benches along rivers and streams, along woodland borders and paths. *S. helvula* is found in similar habitats but will tolerate more open conditions, such as cropland borders, fencerows, and roadsides. Range of both species is the eastern United States and Canada, west to Texas and the Dakotas.

Uses

After hulling the brown skin, hog peanut tubers are edible raw but better if cooked; they are a bit like a single-seeded peanut. The small, aerial beans are also edible raw or cooked, similar to lentils. *S. helvula* has edible beans and roots, best when cooked.

Warnings/Comments

Wild beans should be cooked before consuming in quantity. Hog peanut is fairly common and can be an aggressive colonizer in some conditions. The "peanuts" aren't always present, but occasionally can be found in quantity. There are three similar species of *Strophostyles* in the Ozarks, all with similar uses. Both *A. bracteata* and *S. helvula* were utilized by indigenous peoples; food remains have been found in archaeological excavations of prehistoric sites.

Groundnut leaves and flowers

AMERICAN GROUNDNUT
(AKA HOPNISS, POTATO BEAN, INDIAN POTATO)
Apios americana

Native

Edible: flowers, beans, shoots, tubers

This plant's tasty tubers were heavily utilized by indigenous tribes, and the first European colonists were very fond of them. They have promise as a cultivated crop, and probably would have been cultivated already if not for the somewhat time-consuming process to locate and dig the tubers and their long growth cycle.

Description

This perennial herbaceous vine has a two-year growth cycle and grows to 10'–20'. It lacks tendrils and climbs by entwining itself on other vegetation or structures. Groundnut is unusual among pod-bearing bean vines in this family in that its leaves are not trifoliate. It has alternate, compound leaves that are odd-pinnate with 3–9 leaflets, but 5 is typical. The leaflets are 1½"–3½" long and ¾"–2¼" across, with blades that are lanceolate, oblong-

Groundnuts

lanceolate, or ovate in shape, with smooth margins. The foliage exudes a milky latex when broken. Fragrant, showy flowers form in moderate to thick density on conical racemes; they are red-brown to maroon or purple, with pealike wings and keel. Flowers mature to form cylindrical pods 2"–4" long, each containing several maroon beans that turn brown with age. The shallow root system grows laterally and is fibrous, with rhizomes and tubers. The tubers are arranged at irregular intervals along the rhizomes like knotted ropes. Individual tubers are ½"–3" long and ovoid to globoid in shape; the white interior is covered by a brown skin.

Habitat/Range

Prefers moist habitats and is found in moist to mesic woodlands, thickets, streambanks, sloughs, prairies, meadows, seeps, and edges of ponds, springs, and fens. Range is the eastern United States and Canada, west to Texas and the Dakotas.

Uses

The tubers are an excellent food source with many health benefits and can be harvested any time of the year. They are sweetest when dug in late spring or early fall; second-year tubers get quite a bit larger but have tougher skins. Dig around the base of the vine to find the occasionally-branching strings of rhizomes, then follow them to find the tubers. They have a somewhat bitter latex and contain protease inhibitors that act as antinutrients so must be peeled and cooked to remove those. Some recommend boiling the tubers first; then they can be fried, roasted, or added to cooked dishes. The shoots, beans, and flowers are also edible after cooking.

Warnings/Comments

Some report a negative reaction to consuming the tubers, even after eating them for years with no effects. This could be from undercooking, but it's always best to try a small amount first to gauge your body's reaction. The beans contain up to 30 percent crude protein; the tubers contain about 17 percent. Both contain beneficial amino acids and are being studied in cancer research for their high levels of the anticarcinogenic compound genistein.

GROUND PLUM (AKA MILK VETCH, BUFFALO PEA)
Astragalus crassicarpus

Native

Edible: ripe fruits

My first encounter with ground plum was in an opening on a steep, wooded hillside at my property on the Niangua River, where the ripe plum-colored pods caught my eye. I was eager for a taste after seeing them in a field guide and was amazed at the sweet, snow pea–flavored succulent crunch. I've been a big fan ever since!

Description

Erect or sprawling hairy stems form in small bunches up to 20", each bearing opposite compound leaves. Leaflets are up to ½" long and less than ¼" wide, elliptic, with a blunt or pointed tip. Several 3"–4" flower stalks emerge from the leaf axils, producing up to 12 pea-type flowers in terminal racemes. Individual flowers are about ¾" long with an erect, notched upper petal, and 2 small, horizontal lower petals that are variably white, pink, lavender, or purplish in color. Smooth, light green fruits appear early to late June. They are generally round or oblong, ½"–1" long, with a central ridge, occasionally with a pointed tip, later ripening to pink or light purple. Each contains many small, black kidney-shaped seeds. As they mature, the heavy fruits often droop to the ground, thus the name.

Ground plum flower

Habitat/Range

This perennial is found in prairie and glade habitats, fields, roadside embankments, ledges, tops of bluffs, and in rich and/or dry upland forest openings throughout most of the Ozarks. Its range encompasses prairie habitats and dry slopes in much of the Great Plains, from Montana to Minnesota, south to New Mexico and Texas, and east to the Ozarks.

Uses

Eat the fruits raw on the spot, or slice and add them raw or cooked to any dish, similar to snow peas. They are a delicious addition to wild salads and can be pickled. *Astragalus* root has been used medicinally in Asia for centuries; ongoing studies are confirming many beneficial properties.

Warnings/Comments

Some western species of *Astragalus* are called locoweed, as the leaves contain the toxic glycoside swainsonine. Ingestion of this plant by livestock causes toxic poisoning called locoism, which produces frantic, dazed, and uncoordinated behavior. No similar toxic species have round fruits, but to be safe, ground plums probably should not be consumed in large quantity. This may be difficult, as they are one of the tastiest native wild edibles!

EASTERN REDBUD
Cercis Canadensis

Native

Edible: flowers, leaves, seedpods

Redbud is a welcome harbinger of spring in the Ozarks. Its showy bursts of purplish-pink blossoms dot the brown hillsides just as the misty, pastel green of new leaf growth starts to appear.

Description

A small to medium-size understory tree 12'–40' tall, usually with a crooked, branching trunk and spreading branches. Alternate, long-petioled leaves are 3"–6" long, 2½"–6" wide, orbicular to heart shaped, with a bluish-green, smooth upper surface, pale undersides, and smooth margins. Bark is gray to reddish brown and smooth on younger branches, developing shallow furrows and blocky scales with age. Twigs are smooth and brown, with white lenticels. Young shoots are olive green, often zigzagging with each leaf. Bloom clusters often cover the entire tree in late March–May before foliage emerges. Small buds on twigs and older branches produce umbellate clusters of 2–8 purple–rose pink flowers on ¼" stalks. Individual flowers are 5-petaled, ¼"–½" long, typical of those in the pea family. Flowers are replaced by abundant seedpod clusters. Individual pods look like miniature

Redbud pods

snow peas; they are green and leathery with tapered ends, 3"–4" long, ½" wide, each containing 6–10 flattened, oval ¼" seeds. Pods will dry to brown and often persist into winter.

Habitat/Range
Found in open woodlands and borders, forested slopes, dolomite glades, rocky streambanks, bluffs, fencerows, wooded bottoms, and valleys above flood line. Occurs throughout the eastern United States and southern Midwest, west to eastern Texas and Kansas, north to the southern Great Lakes. Absent from most of the coastal areas and New England.

Uses
Raw flowers are a great trail nibble or addition to salads, and they make good jelly. To harvest, pluck the unopened buds and flowers by the stems without disturbing the twig bud. (Removing the bud will inhibit future blooms.) Young, tender leaves can be added to salad greens. Young pods can be eaten raw, steamed, pickled, or added to stir-fries, soups, and other cooked dishes, but have a fairly short period of edibility before becoming tough and fibrous.

Warnings/Comments
Flowers are reported to be high in vitamin C. Seedpods contain 25 percent protein, 8 percent fat, and 3 percent ash. A 2006 study determined that flowers and seeds were high in antioxidants and anthocyanins, as well as linoleic and alpha-linolenic acids. Often planted as an ornamental.

RECIPE

Redbud Flower Jelly

1¾ cups redbud infusion (see below)

2 tablespoons fresh lemon juice

3½ cups sugar

⅛ teaspoon butter

1 pouch Certo fruit pectin

1. To make the infusion, bring 2 cups water to a boil. Remove from heat and add red-bud flowers (about 2 cups); cover. Let sit for 10 minutes then strain through layers of damp cheesecloth or a fine wire strainer.

2. Measure 1¾ cups (exact measurement) of prepared infusion into a 6- to 8-quart pot. Add lemon juice and sugar, plus ⅛ teaspoon butter to reduce foaming. Bring to a rolling boil on high heat while stirring. Stir in pectin and boil for 1 minute, stirring constantly.

3. Remove from heat and skim off any foam. Ladle quickly into prepared jars filled within ¼" of the tops. Clean rims and threads, and fully tighten two-piece lids. Allow to cool and then refrigerate. (Boil jars and lids in a water bath before filling to store unrefrigerated.) Works well with violet flowers or any sweet and colorful flower petals.

FAGACEAE (BEECHES, OAKS)

This family of deciduous or evergreen trees and shrubs comprises about 927 species in 8 genera and is characterized by alternate simple leaves with pinnate venation, unisexual flowers in the form of catkins, and fruit in the form of capped nuts. Many oaks can grow to attain great size. One specimen of live oak on John's Island in South Carolina, called the "Angel Oak," has a trunk circumference of 28 feet, with branches up to 187 feet long.

White oak acorns and leaves

OAKS
Quercus spp.

Native

Edible: acorns

Acorns were among the most heavily-utilized plant foods by indigenous peoples. Even though the process to make them edible was time-consuming, their high protein and fat content, long storage life, and easy collection made them a diet staple wherever people encountered them. Commercial acorn flour is expensive to buy—if you can locate or afford it—but those willing to put in the processing time can produce their own tasty, gluten-free grain alternative.

Description

Quercus species are split into two general groups, white oaks and red oaks. The white oak group is usually preferred for acorn harvest because of lower tannin levels, but all can be used after processing; red oaks just require much more processing to remove the tannins. The leaves of the two groups can be differentiated easily. Leaves of the red oak group have small, sharp pins on the outer points, or lobes, of leaf margins. Leaves of the white oak group have rounded or pointed lobes, without pins. Acorns of red oaks also tend to have flatter caps. *Q. macrocarpa* (bur oak) trees have the largest acorns and tend to have the lowest amounts of tannins.

Bur oak leaves and acorn PHOTO BY ROCKY HOLLOW

Uses

To begin processing, put the acorns in a bucket of water. The good ones will sink to the bottom; pick out and discard the floaters. The next step is to leach the bitter tannins. The most common methods use either hot water or cold water; both were used by indigenous tribes. After leaching, acorns can be used as any nut or made into a highly nutritious flour. Hot-water leaching is better if you plan on using the broken bits as nuts.

Cold-water leaching is best for making flour because it retains more of the nutrients. First remove the hulls and brown skins covering the meats. Boiling them beforehand can make this task easier. Keep the peeled acorns in water until right before processing to prevent oxidization. If you're making flour, the acorns should be ground up with a *molcajete* or a food processor then mixed with a bit of water to make a slurry. Fill quart jars half full with the resulting thick liquid, then cover the rest of the way with water. Agitate periodically, then allow to sit and settle; the mush will settle to the bottom. Pour off the water at the top through cheesecloth to save any bits, then fill again with fresh water. Repeat this daily for 5–10 days until the bitterness is gone. The final stage will be separated into the grit at the bottom, a thin layer of cream, and a top layer of acorn milk. Pour through double layers of cheesecloth, saving the nut milk, and squeeze as much liquid from the grit to make drying easier. Dry the grit without heat; once dried, it can be used as flour or stored. The nut milk can be boiled to a ⅓ reduction then sweetened for drinking or used in soups or as a thickener. A field method of leaching is to place the mush into fine-mesh net bags then put into a stream of moving water for several days to a week.

For hot leaching, place the acorn bits into a pot of boiling water till the water turns a dark tea color; this is repeated till the water is mostly clear, usually 4–6 times. Always start with boiling water; putting the acorns into water and then bringing it to a boil can set the bitter flavor.

I recently learned about a couple of processing methods I've yet to try. The first is to put the mush into several foot-long bottom segments of ladies' nylon hose then hang them in the upper tank of your toilet for several days. The repeated flushing of the fresh water will leach the tannins. It may sound disgusting to some, but it is perfectly safe— toilet tank water is listed as an emergency water source in many survival manuals. Fermenting, salt brine, or dry-salt curing processes similar to those used for olives may be alternative ways to remove the tannins from whole acorns. These methods work well with red oak group acorns and others with higher levels of tannins as ways to preserve their higher fat content.

Below is a list of the most common oaks found in the Ozarks. Specific ID is often difficult, as there is much hybridization within and even between groups. Fat and protein content vary widely among species; some in the red oak group have higher fat content and were sought after to make oil.

WHITE OAK GROUP SPECIES:

White oak (*Q. alba*), post oak (*Q. stellate*), bur oak (*Q. macrocarpa*), chinquapin oak (*Q. muhlenbergii*)

RED OAK GROUP SPECIES:

Northern red oak (*Q. rubra*), southern red oak (*Q. falcate*), black oak (*Q. veutina*), blackjack oak (*Q. marilandica*), shingle oak (*Q. imbricaria*)

Warnings/Comments

All acorns must be leached before consuming, even those that aren't particularly bitter. Acorns contain phytic and tannic acids; both act as antinutrients that bind with beneficial minerals and nutrients, preventing the gut from absorbing them.

GROSSULARIACEAE (GOOSEBERRIES)

This family has about 150 species of shrubs in 2 distinct groups, the currants and the gooseberries. They are native to temperate North America, extending southward into the Andes. Currants usually lack spines and have clustered flowers; gooseberries are usually prickly, with solitary flowers.

MISSOURI GOOSEBERRY
Ribes missouriense

Native

Edible: berries

Description

A deciduous shrub up to 4' tall, usually round in shape with multiple thorny stems, occasionally forming large colonies. Older stems are gray to brown, erect to arching, prickly, with 1–3 larger spines at leaf nodes. Young stems are green, hairy or prickly, occasionally smooth. Alternate leaves occur up the stems in bunches of 2–3 leaves. Each leaf is up to 2" across, generally round in shape, with 3–5 broadly-toothed primary lobes that are rounded at the tips and wedge-shaped at the base. White or pale green blooms appear April–May, consisting of 2–3 small, drooping flowers emerging on short racemes at the leaf axils. Each flower consists of a narrow, tubular calyx and 4–5 narrow, often reflexed lobes, with 5 stamens that extend far out of the calyx. Fertilized flowers mature in early summer into round green berries up to ⅓" across, ripening to dark purple. Each contains numerous dark seeds.

Habitat/Range
Found in open, mesic or dry rocky woods and their borders, thickets, old fields, glades, power line cuts, and partially shaded fencerows. Range is eastern and midwestern United States, west to Oklahoma and the Dakotas, south to Arkansas and Tennessee, and east to Virginia and New York. Absent from much of New England.

Uses
The green berries are a tart, refreshing trail nibble, although some prefer them ripe and sweet. Ripe or green berries can be used in preserves, syrups, sauces, and juices and can be dried or frozen for later use. The tart flavor of green berries is preferred in pies, cobblers, and jam with the addition of a sugar or sweetener of choice.

Warnings/Comments
Some people report a dermatitis rash when coming in contact with the spines. Gooseberry is an attractive native suitable for edible landscaping. *Ribes cynosbati* (eastern prickly gooseberry) is similar but has soft prickles on the fruit and is less common. *Ribes aureum* (golden or clove currant) has yellow flowers that smell similar to cloves and lacks spines. Fruit is golden yellow, orange-red, brown, or black.

JUGLANDACEAE (HICKORIES, WALNUTS)

Valued for both their wood and their nuts, this family consists of about 50 species of trees or shrubs in 10 genera. *Juglans regia* (Persian walnut) is one of the major nut crops of the world; *Juglans nigra* (black walnut) is one of the most economically valuable trees in the Ozarks.

HICKORIES
Mockernut leaf and nut Carya spp.

Native

Edible: nuts

Southern pecan pie, hickory-smoked meat, ax handles, and longbows are examples of the usefulness of hickories. The nuts of several species rival pecan in flavor.

Description

Hickories are medium to large, straight-trunked trees, typically with short, stout limbs and a narrow crown. All have alternate, compound leaves that are

Mockernut meat

Shagbark trunk

Pecan leaves and nuts

odd-pinnate and 8"–20" long. Leaflets are lanceolate to broadly ovate, 3"–8" long, usually glossy, with serrated margins. There are eight *Carya* species in the Ozarks, forming two groups. *C. illinoiensis* (pecan) and *C. cordiformus* (bitternut) are members of the pecan hickories, with 7–17 leaflets and flattened, elongated terminal buds. *C. ovata* (shagbark), *C. laciniosa* (shellbark), *C. tomentosa* (mockernut), *C. glabra* (pignut), and *C. texana* (black hickory) are members of the true hickories, with 5–7 leaflets and either small or large egg-shaped terminal buds. A mature shagbark hickory is one of the easiest trees to identify by its bark, which peels from the tree in long, shaggy, often curved strips or plates.

Uses

Use as any other nut. Extracting the nutmeats can be time-consuming, as the shell chambers can be smaller or more convoluted than in other tree nuts. A nutpick or dental pick is helpful. First remove the husks; an easy way is to store them till they dry and open on their own. Put the nuts in a container of water, and remove the bad ones that float. Boiling or baking the hulled nuts can make them easier to crack. Another way to process is to crack the shells thoroughly into small bits and cover with boiling water in a container. The shells sink and the nutmeats float, allowing them to be skimmed off the water's surface. Indigenous people made *pawcohiccora*, a hickory nut milk made by pulverizing shell and all, boiling the mush until thick and creamy, then filtering out the shells. Fire-roasting the nuts can give a nice smoky flavor. The cambium of many species makes a very strong wrapping or cordage fiber.

Habitat/Range
Commonly found in most upland and bottomland forested habitats. Native to eastern North America.

Warnings/Comments
Shagbark, shellbark, mockernut, and pecan are the tastiest species; others species are edible but can be bitter. Native tribes left behind many "nutting stones," used to hold the nut in place while being cracked. A chert hammer-stone was used to peck a small depression into the flat surface of a piece of sandstone or other soft stone; some were pecked right into bedrock. They do make cracking nuts much easier!

RECIPE

Shagbark Hickory Syrup

1 pound shagbark hickory bark pieces

Water

Sugar

1. Preheat oven to 350°F.

2. Rinse bark thoroughly in plain water (scrub if needed); discard pieces with lichens on them. Spread the pieces on a flat pan and roast for 20–30 minutes. When finished roasting, bark should have a sweet-smoky aroma.

3. Put the pieces in a large pot and cover with water; bring to a boil then simmer for 30–40 minutes. Remove the bark and strain the liquid. Measure liquid then return it to the pot. Add an equal amount of sugar; bring to a boil. Reduce heat to a simmer; cook until the volume is reduced by 25 to 30 percent, whisking to avoid scorching.

4. Cool; decant into bottles or jars.

BLACK WALNUT, BUTTERNUT
Juglans nigra, J. cinerea

Native

Edible: nuts

Description

Black walnut is a large, straight-trunked tree to 100' with a rounded, open crown. Trunk bark is dark gray to nearly black with deep furrows; branch bark is grayish and smooth. Alternate compound leaves are up to 2' long, odd-bipinnate with 11–23 leaflets, with a terminal leaflet often smaller than the side leaflets. Each leaflet is smooth, lanceolate or ovoid-lanceolate, up to 3" long and 1" across, with serrated margins. Flowers April–May, with male catkins and female florets on the same tree.

Female flowers mature to green globoid nuts up to 2½" across, forming either singly or in pairs. The husks ripen to splotchy yellow-black and wrinkled when they start to drop in September–October, eventually becoming black and mushy with staining oils. The woody, ridged nut inside has 4 interior chambers containing aromatic nutmeats.

Habitat/Range

Found in rich, well-drained soils, bottomlands, benches along streams, bases of bluffs, valleys, mesic woodlands in association with ash, hickory, maple, and oak. Range is the eastern and midwestern United States and Canada, west to Texas and the Dakotas. May be present or introduced in most western states.

Uses

The nutmeats can be used as any other nut. Use them in sweet breads, ice cream, and confections. To dehull, mash them with your foot and pick out the nut; gloves are handy to avoid staining your hands. To dehull large amounts, lay them in your driveway; vehicle tires will squish the hull and leave the hard nuts to be easily picked out. Once hulled, cure/

Butternut, with nutmeat BUTTERNUT PHOTO BY RYAN HAWKINS

dry them for a couple weeks in a cool, dry place with ventilation. Afterward, they can be stored shelled or unshelled. The hulls can be used to make a fast dye for fabric and leather. They also have extensive medicinal properties. Hulls contain the compound juglone, which is toxic to fish and was used by indigenous tribes as a fish poison in still waters. That particular use is illegal, but I knew a couple of guys back when . . .

Warnings/Comments

Missouri is the largest producer of black walnuts, leading to its designation as the Missouri state nut tree. Its voluminous nut production for harvest and beautiful, dark heartwood make it our most economically valuable tree. The roots produce a compound that inhibits nearby growth. The similar *J. cinerea* (butternut) has pale gray or light brown bark; nuts are cylindrical and brown, with sweeter nutmeats than black walnut. It is declining across its range due to a fungal disease.

LAMIACEAE (MINTS)

This large, globally-distributed family consists of about 7,000 species in 236 genera. Many species are cultivated commercially for their colorful leaves and flowers; others are grown for their fragrance and medicinal properties and for use in tea. Mints characteristically have square stems and simple, opposite leaves, and many have 2-lipped open-mouthed tubular flowers. Some species have the aromatic, mint smell; others do not. Most are used as teas or flavorings; milder species are good salad ingredients.

NON-AROMATIC MINTS

Edible: green upper parts, flowers

PHOTO BY DEBORAH TYLER

HENBIT, PURPLE DEADNETTLE, GROUND IVY
Lamium amplexicaule, L. purpureum, Glechoma hederacea

Introduced

Edible: leaves, flowers, stems

Description

Henbit is a low-growing annual that often forms bright pinkish-purple carpets in fields when blooming. Multiple stems are slender, erect or decumbent, branching, 2"–3" tall. Opposite leaves are orbicular or with shallow palmate lobes and scalloped margins. Lower leaves are 1" across and on petioles; smaller upper leaves clasp the stem near the flowers.

PHOTO BY DEBORAH TYLER

Dead nettle   Ground ivy

Blooms February–November, with flowers occurring in whorls at leaf axils and stem termi-
nals. Tiny flower buds are deep red when first forming, maturing to ½" erect flowers, each
with a lavender to purplish tubular corolla and hood-shaped upper lip and 2 pale lower
petals. *L. purpureum* (purple deadnettle) is a similar, related species often found with henbit. It has similar flowers, with purplish, triangular leaves that are on petioles. *Glechoma
hederacea* (gill-over-the-ground, ground ivy, creeping Charlie) is similar to henbit, but it
has round to reniform leaves with palmate venation and larger, blue flowers, each with a
small upper lobe, large lower lobe, and 2 smaller side lobes.

Habitat/Range
All 3 species are common in fields, pastures, gardens, cropland borders, and yards and
near buildings. Prefers moist, fertile soils in disturbed or open ground. Native to Eurasia
and Africa; introduced throughout the United States and Canada.

Uses

Mints without the minty taste, the mild-tasting young leaves and stems of all three species are good in salads or pesto; can be briefly cooked as a potherb or in stir-fries or added to soups and other cooked dishes.

Warnings/Comments

Ground ivy can be toxic to horses. All *Lamiaceae* and related species are edible and are used similarly. All have square stems, but there are other square-stemmed plants that aren't related.

AROMATIC MINTS

Edible: Leaves, flowers, in salads, teas, and seasonings.

ARKANSAS CALAMINT
Clinopodium arkansanum

Native

Description

A feathery and delicate perennial usually less than 1' tall, often forming dense mats. Opposite leaves are up to 1" long, linear, with smooth margins. Smaller secondary and even-smaller tertiary leaves appear at leaf axils, giving it a whorled appearance. Pale lavender flowers are ½" long, trumpet-shaped, with 2 upper and 3 lower lobes. All upper parts have a very strong, almost burning scent and flavor.

Habitat/Range

Found in open pristine habitats, on exposed limestone bedrock, glades or outcrops, and open, rocky areas with thin soil. Range is mostly Missouri and Arkansas, extending west to New Mexico and Kansas and northeast to the Great Lakes states.

Uses

Calamint is the one of the strongest mints, excellent for teas and in mojitos. During the 1980s I was conducting bird and plant fieldwork in hot, open glades, and the water in my backpack had become so warm that it was hard to drink. I stuffed a few sprigs of calamint into the water bottle, making a cooling, strong tea that almost burned my throat like ice water. It was much better and more refreshing than drinking plain hot water!

Warnings/Comments

Avoid consuming during pregnancy; some sources report this plant to be a uterine stimulant.

This inconspicuous plant is often first detected by aroma rather than sight. Walking through a patch will fill the air with a delightful minty fragrance. The aroma is largely due to menthol, and the crushed leaves can be rubbed on the skin to repel insects.

Arkansas Calamint is common in the southern half of Missouri and in northern Arkansas, but it is relatively scarce outside that region. As of early 2019, there is no record for this plant in Missouri north of the Missouri River.

DITTANY
Cunila origanoides

Native

Description
A low-growing woodland species up to 1½" tall, with sparse, paired leaves on slender, stiff stems and small, purplish-blue flowers at the leaf axils and stem terminus.

Habitat/Range
Found in dry upland woods, borders of woodlands and prairies, and wooded slopes; prefers acidic soils. Range is eastern and lower midwestern United States.

Uses
Dittany has a distinct oregano smell/taste with peppery overtones. Best as a savory flavoring; use in pesto, soups, and other dishes in place of oregano.

Warnings/Comments
During the first frosts of winter, dittany is one of several plants that produce a phenomenon popularly known as "frost flowers." This is where watery sap is pushed out of stem cracks near the base and becomes frozen in crystalline ribbon-like projections, often becoming curled and resembling flower petals. It is also used medicinally in folk remedies for fever and headaches. As with all strong-flavored mints, avoid consumption during pregnancy.

HAIRY MOUNTAIN MINT
Pycnanthemum pilosum

Native

Description
A slender, bushy mint up to 3' tall, with a much-branched stem, pale greenish-white pubescent leaves and stem, and clusters of white flowers at the stem terminus.

Habitat/Range
Found in open, dry woodlands, old fields, thickets, and prairies. Range is the central-midwestern United States, east to New York and Georgia, west to Nebraska and Texas.

Uses
Hairy mountain mint has a strong, almost burning mint smell and taste, similar to calamint. It is excellent in teas, cocktails, and other beverages. Some add it to smoke mixtures.

Warnings/Comments
This plant is a pollinator magnet as blooms appear in midsummer, when it attracts a large variety of native butterflies, bees, and wasps. Its beauty, ease of growing from seed, and tendency to grow in clumps instead of spreading by runners can make it a good choice for ornamental flower gardens. *P. tenufolium* (Slender Mountain Mint) is similar but with hairless, narrow leaves and dense branching, giving it a weedy appearance. As with all strong-flavored mints, avoid consuming during pregnancy.

PERILLA (AKA BEEFSTEAK MINT, SHISO, WILD BASIL, RATTLESNAKE WEED)
Perilla frutescens

Introduced

Description
A weedy, branched annual to 3' tall, appearing structurally similar to cultivated garden coleus. Leaves are up to 3" wide and 5" long, on short petioles, with coarsely-toothed margins. Leaf color can be green, purple, burgundy, and any shade in between. Small purple flowers form in August–October on upright racemes up to 6" long. Dry seed capsules often rattle in the wind and persist into winter.

Habitat/Range
Found in gardens, lawn borders, pastures, moist or dry wooded bottomlands, disturbed waste areas; along streambanks, gravel bars, and woodland trails. Introduced from Asia.

Uses
A very useful plant, commonly used as *shiso* in Asian cuisine. Good when used sparingly in salads. The mint/licorice/cinnamon flavor adds zest to rice, pasta, soups; any raw or cooked dish. Leaves and flower buds can be fried in tempura, added to pickled items, packed in salt for bouillon, and used to make *shiso* oil for drizzles and cooking. The seeds can be sprouted.

Warnings/Comments
Humans have been consuming perilla for thousands of years with no ill effects, but the plant contains ketones that can be fatally toxic to livestock.

WILD BERGAMOT (AKA HORSEMINT)
Monarda fistulosa

Native

Description
A tall, branched perennial, up to 4' tall. Leaves are lanceolate to ovate, up to 4" long, with serrated margins. Flowerheads up to 3" across form at the stem terminus; showy individual flowers are pink to pale lavender, about 1" long, tubular, with extended stamens and 3 drooping petals.

Habitat/Range
Found in prairies, savannas, fields, roadsides, woodland borders, glades, and along road-sides. Range is most of the United States and southern Canada. Absent from Florida and California.

Uses
Bergamot has a similar but milder flavor than dittany; it is great for food seasoning and teas. Add to black tea, chicory/dandelion root tea, or New Jersey tea (*Ceanothus americanus*) to make mock Earl Grey.

Warnings/Comments
As with all strong-flavored mints, avoid consuming during pregnancy. Wild bergamot is a great addition to ornamental flower gardens. Its large, attractive blooms are irresistible to a wide range of pollinating insects.

FIELD MINT
Mentha arvense and other *Mentha* spp.

Native and Introduced

Description
Native and introduced varieties and hybrids of this perennial herb can be found in both hemispheres. It is an erect or sprawling herb up to 1½' tall, with leaves that are up to 2½" long, broadly lanceolate to ovate, with prominent veins and serrated margins. Whorled flower clusters appear above the leaf axils on the upper stem or at the stem terminus.

Habitat/Range

Found in rich, moist conditions along springs; in borders of marshes, fens, and lakes; wet prairies; and disturbed ground.

Uses

Hybrids and varieties of *Mentha* species are known for the classic mint, spearmint, and peppermint flavor found in teas, candies, and other minty delights such as mint julep and mojito cocktails.

Warnings/Comments

The health benefits of consuming plants in the mint family is apparently not limited to humans and other mammals. Scientific studies have recorded increases in growth performance and immune function when mint oils were included in the diets of two fish species, Caspian whitefish (*Rutilus frisii kutum*), and Caspian brown trout (*Salmo trutta caspius*).

RECIPE

Three-wild-mint Dolmas

Fresh perilla leaves (the largest you can find)

Dittany or wild bergamot

Field mint

Wood sorrel

Purslane (or any available flavorful greens)

Cooked rice

Shelled pumpkin seeds (or any available wild seeds or nuts)

1. Preheat oven to 175 degrees.

2. Crush the seeds/nuts with a small bit of chopped dittany, wood sorrel, and sweet mint. Make a sweet version with dates or wild fruits, or make it savory with cooked and seasoned ground meats and feta or other dry cheese.

3. Mix the nut mixture with the meats/fruits and rice and a pinch of salt; roll up inside the perilla leaves.

4. Place in a rectangular pan; drizzle with balsamic vinegar and a bit of olive oil. Bake for 10 minutes.

MALVACEAE (MALLOWS)

This family is composed of about 4,225 known species in 244 genera, including economically important species such as okra, cotton, cacao, hibiscus, and durian. Its members occur worldwide except in the coldest habitats but are most common in the tropics.

COMMON MALLOW
(AKA DWARF MALLOW, CHEESEWEED)
Malva neglecta

Introduced

Edible: leaves, stems, flowers, seeds

Description

A low-growing annual with roundish leaves and multiple, erect to prostrate stems that emerge from a taproot. Stems are usually vine-like with white hairs, up to 3' but usually smaller. Alternate, crinkled leaves appear on long petioles and are 2½" long and 3" wide or larger, orbicular to reniform, with a deeply indented base and 5–9 shallow lobes with wavy and crenate margins. Blooms April–October, with 1–4 flowers appearing on short peduncles above the leaf axils. Flowers are ¾" across, with 5 white, pink, or pale violet longitudinally-striped petals emerging from a short 5-lobed calyx. The central reproductive column consists of a single pistil and numerous appressed stamens. Flowers develop into button-like flattened discoid fruits, each with 12–15 seeds encircling the outer edge.

Habitat/Range
Found mostly in disturbed ground with moderate to rich soil; in gardens, croplands, barnyards, vacant lots, roadsides, edges of yards and paths. Native to Europe; introduced throughout the United States and Canada. Absent from Louisiana, Mississippi, and Florida.

Uses
Use young, tender leaves, flowers, chopped stems, and green seeds as a mild-flavored salad addition. All tender upper parts can be cooked as greens or added to soups and other cooked dishes. The green seeds can be pickled for use as capers. Like its cultivated relative okra, all parts of the plant develop a slight mucilaginous quality when cooked. After winnowing, mature seeds can be cooked like rice, roasted and added to seedcakes, or pickled and used as capers. Used medicinally to treat a number of ailments, the mucilaginous properties of mallow tea help relieve throat and stomach irritation. The root can be boiled to make a thickener or added to soups, but it is often too fibrous to eat.

Warnings/Comments
Fertilized, nitrogen-rich soil near croplands or in gardens may cause high nitrate concentrations in the leaves; it's best to consume in small quantities when collected in those conditions, or just limit harvest to wild conditions. The root of a related species, *Althea officinalis* (marsh mallow), was boiled with honey to make a confection in ancient Egypt and was the origin of our sugary, puffed-gelatin treat by the same name.

BASSWOOD (AKA AMERICAN LINDEN, LIME TREE)
Tilia americana

Native

Edible: leaves, shoots, buds, flowers, nuts, cambium
It's not often you find a tree with so many edible, medicinal, and utilitarian uses. It also has beautiful flowers that waft sweet fragrance across the water during my favorite pastime—a float trip down a beautiful, clear Ozarks stream. (If you hear banjos, paddle faster!)

Description
A medium-size tree with a broad, spreading crown, 50'–100' at maturity. Trunk bark is gray, with longitudinal flat, scaly ridges, and deep and brownish furrows. Young twigs are zigzagged, green to brown, turning gray with age, with numerous lenticels. Winter buds are red. Alternate, simple leaves are 4"–6" long and 3"–5" wide, generally cordate or ovate-orbicular with a pointed tip, often with the base rounded on one side and flat on

the other. Margins are coarsely toothed. Upper blade surface is shiny dark green; undersurface is paler with small hairy tufts at vein axils. Fragrant blooms appear late May–August, with long stalks forming at leaf axils. Each stalk is attached mid-length to 1 or several strap-like floral bracts about 3"–5" long and 1" wide that terminate in drooping cymes of 6–15 white to pale yellow 5-petaled flowers. Each flower is approximately ½" across, maturing to a dry, spherical ¼" nutlet in August–October.

Habitat/Range

Found in wooded bottoms, moist bases of wooded slopes, ravines, bases of bluffs, and along streams and rivers. Range is throughout the eastern and midwestern United States, west to North Dakota and Texas; introduced into much of eastern Canada.

Uses

Shoots, buds, and young tender leaves are great raw in salads, boiled as greens, or added to soups and other cooked dishes. Larger tender leaves can be used to wrap dolmas. Flowers can be added to salads or used with leaves to make a highly medicinal tea for treatment of coughs, colds, insomnia, and high blood pressure. In the spring, the cambium has a cucumber-like flavor when eaten raw. It also can be added to soups or breads or dried and powdered for later use. The small seeds are edible after removing the outer hull. The cambium also makes a superior cordage fiber. The soft, light wood is preferred by woodcarvers, and is among the best materials for the spindle and hearth in bow-drill fire making.

Warnings/Comments

Red mulberry (*Morus rubra*) has leaves that can appear similar, but its leaves produce a milky sap; often has single or double-lobed leaves on the same tree. The name basswood is a corruption of "bast wood," from the common use of its cambium as a cordage fiber, also known as "bast."

MORACEAE (MULBERRIES)

This mostly tropical or subtropical family has over 1,100 species in 38 genera, and includes other edible species such as fig, banyan, and breadfruit. A regionally local, related species is the native *Maclura pomifera* (Osage orange, Bois d' Arc, hedgeapple), whose strange-looking large, green fruits have edible seeds; its wood is the premier material for bowmakers.

PHOTO BY ROCKY HOLLOW

RED MULBERRY
Morus rubra

Native

Edible: fruits, leaves

Description

A fast-growing, small to medium-size tree up to 60' with a stout trunk and a rounded, branched crown. Trunk bark of larger trees is thin, grayish to brown, with shallow furrows and slight, flat ridges. Branch bark is brown, reddish brown, or gray, and smooth. Twigs have sparse lenticels with smooth, green shoots. Alternate leaves form abundantly on twigs and shoots; all bleed milky sap. Leaves are 3"–6" long, up to 4" wide, simple with serrated margins, usually oval to ovate, but often with 3–5 moderate to deep lobes, a rounded base, and pointed tip. Flowers appear in April–May; can be either dioecious or monoecious, with male catkins 2"–3" long, female catkins 1" or less. Female catkins develop into cylindrical, aggregate fruits (resembling blackberries) up to 1¼" long that ripen to red or purplish black in June–August.

Habitat/Range

Found in floodplain valleys and woodlands, moist upland wooded slopes and their borders, fencerows, glades; planted ornamentally in parks and yards. Range is the eastern United States and Ontario, west to Texas and South Dakota, east to Florida and Massachusetts. For unknown reasons, it appears to be declining across parts of its range.

Uses

Packed with resveratrol, vitamins, and antioxidants, mulberries are a great nutritious snack when eaten on the spot; can be used in pies, pastries, breads, muffins, sorbet, wine, syrup, and meat sauces. The berries deteriorate quickly after harvest, so use quickly or dry or freeze for later use. Taste can vary within individual trees, some better than others. Young, tender leaves can be mixed with other potherbs or dried for teas. The wood is good for making bows. The cambium layer of young shoots makes a strong cordage fiber. Various parts of the plants are used medicinally for a number of conditions.

Warnings/Comments

The unripe fruits and mature leaves of *M. rubra* and other related species contain toxins that can cause a range of symptoms when eaten in excess, such as mild euphoria, hallucinations, stomach distress, and diarrhea. *R. alba* (white mulberry) was cultivated 4,000 years ago in China and is now naturalized in the United States and across the globe as the preferred host plant for silkworm (*Bombyx mori*) production. *Broussonetia papyrifera* (paper mulberry), another Asian species, has become aggressively invasive in the United States.

NELUMBONACEAE (LOTUSES)

Formerly included within Nymphaeaceae (water lilies), Nelumbonaceae now consists of a single genus with two species. *N. lutea* occurs in North America; *N. nucifera* (sacred lotus) is found in Asia. Both species are rhizomatous aquatic plants that are rooted in soil in shallow slow or still water. Like Nymphaeaceae, they have large, showy flowers and large round leaves on long petioles that either float or are suspended above the water's surface.

AMERICAN LOTUS (AKA WATER CHINQUAPIN)
Nelumbo lutea

Native

Edible: leaves, root, stem shoots, seeds
Although cattails have earned the nickname "nature's supermarket," lotus could also claim the title with its sweet root, nutritious seeds, and vegetable-like leaves.

Description

A colony-forming emergent-aquatic plant with large, concave-centered round leaves and showy yellow flowers. Rhizomes rooted in water-covered soil or mud produce long petioles, each connected to the center of a single bluish-green leaf with drooping wavy edges that is 1'–2½' across. Young leaves float at the water surface; mature leaves are held 1'–2' above the surface. Large pale yellow flowers appear in July–September; each is up to 8" across, with 10–20 tepals, golden stamens, and a central yellow receptacle that matures to a flat-topped seed head resembling a showerhead. It contains 10–20 round, hard-shelled and nutlike seeds encased in hollow chambers. The seed head eventually turns brown and droops to release seeds into the water.

Habitat/Range

Prefers slow or still water with mud bottoms. Found in ponds, sloughs, oxbow lakes, shallow lake inlets, marshes, and wetlands with open water. Range is the eastern and midwestern United States and Canada, west to Texas and Nebraska; also occurs in California.

Uses

Freshly unfurled young leaves and stem shoots can be cooked like spinach; older leaves can be used to wrap other foods for baking. Harvest the nutritious seeds while still young and green by shelling and removing the small, bitter embryo. Eat raw or roasted, candied, cooked like peas, dried and ground into flour, or boiled and mashed as a cereal. The starchy banana-shaped tuber can be harvested in the fall. The flavor is similar to sweet potato when baked and is popular in Asian-style stir-fries and soups. The hollow air chambers within the root give it a wagon-wheel appearance when sliced into rounds.

Warnings/Comments

An aggressive colonizer of ponds and waterways, often choking out other aquatic vegetation.

NYMPHAEACEAE (WATER LILIES)

This family contains 5 genera with about 70 known species and is found in temperate and tropical climates around the world. Water lilies are rhizomatous, usually rooted in soil in bodies of water, with leaves and flowers floating on or emergent from the surface. The leaves are round, with a radial notch in *Nymphaea* and *Nuphar*. Its flowers can be small and globe shaped or large and showy.

Yellow pond lily

YELLOW POND LILY (AKA SPATTERDOCK)
Nuphar advena

Native

Edible: leaves, flowers and buds, seeds

Description

Leaves are 6"–12" long, oval or heart shaped with a cleft base, usually floating at or held just above the water's surface. Its yellow, globe-shaped flowers are at or held just above the water's surface, are up to 3" across, usually with 3 outer green and 3 inner yellow sepals that are overlapping and much larger than the many small yellow petals. A large, compound central ovary is surrounded by many stamens. As the flower matures, it forms an attractive urn-shaped seed capsule with a red outer rim.

Habitat/Range

As its name implies, this plant is particularly fond of ponds but can be found in nearly any still or slow-moving body of water that has a shallow, mud bottom. Range is eastern North America, west to Texas and Kansas.

Uses

Fresh leaves and young flower buds can be used as a potherb or added to soups and other dishes. The flowers can be used for tea, and the seeds were heavily utilized by indigenous peoples. According to Green Deane, the best way to process them is to soak the pods in water to rot for three weeks for easier removal and to remove tannins and bitterness. The seeds can then be popped (somewhat) and cooked as a cereal or ground into flour.

Warnings/Comments

Nymphaea spp. (water lilies) have round, floating leaves up to 1' across with a cleft base, and large showy white or pink flowers, each with 20–30 petals. Uses are similar to pond lily, but its seeds are larger and better for popping. *Nymphaea tuberosa* (white water lily) is similar and has edible tubers.

PHOTO BY DEBORAH JOLLY

Water lily

ONAGRACEAE (EVENING PRIMROSES)

This widespread family consists of about 650 species in 17 genera. It occurs on every continent except Antarctica, from boreal to tropical habitats. Many species have showy 4-petaled flowers that are popular ornamental species, such as fuchsia.

COMMON EVENING PRIMROSE (AKA EVENING STAR, SUNDROP, KING'S CURE-ALL)
Oenothera biennis

Native

Edible: leaves, shoots, flowers, buds, roots, seeds
The healthful and medicinal benefits alone should make this mild, somewhat peppery-tasting plant a welcome addition to your foraged goodies.

Description
A night-blooming, erect and leafy biennial up to 6' with showy yellow flowers, often forming colonies. First-year growth emerges from a taproot as a basal rosette; basal leaves are lanceolate, with slightly dentate to serrate margins. Second-year flowering plants are variable, with 1 or more pale green to reddish central stalks, either branched or unbranched. Alternate leaves are densely packed on the stem, with smaller secondary leaves often forming at the leaf axil. Each primary leaf is up to 7" long and 2" wide, lanceolate, sessile, or on short petioles, with smooth to slightly dentate margins. Blooms June–October, with flower clusters forming on racemes at the stem apex and branch terminus. Each flower is roughly 1" across, with 4 pale yellow petals, several protruding stamens, and a long green calyx. Seed capsules are long and thin, containing numerous tiny brown seeds that are often wind-dispersed.

Habitat/Range
Found in prairies, pastures, old fields, glades, bluff openings, gardens, roadsides, power line cuts, cropland borders, old fields, and edges of upland or bottomland forests. Range is throughout the United States and Canada; more common in the eastern half of the United States. Absent from Idaho, Wyoming, Colorado, Utah, and Arizona.

Uses

The sweet flowers, flower buds, and young basal rosette leaves can be eaten raw in salads or added to cooked dishes. Flower stalk leaves are best as a boiled potherb. Young shoots of the flowering stalk can be peeled and eaten raw or cooked. First-year roots can be gathered all year but are best in spring. They can be peppery when eaten raw but are milder when boiled or cooked; can be added to boiled potatoes or other milder vegetables. Some say they are similar to parsnips in flavor and are a good candidate for pickling. There seems to be a lot of regional variability in flavor. If the roots are too pungent for your taste, grind the cooked root and mix with a bit of water, vinegar, and salt to use as a horseradish-like condiment. Young seed pods are edible and have a number of uses. After roasting or baking, they can be used like sesame or poppy seeds. They can be baked in breads, sprinkled into salads

Evening primrose shoot at collection stage

and soups, or steamed and added to other vegetables for a tasty side dish. All parts of the plant have been used medicinally for a number of ailments. The dried flower stalk makes a good hand-drill for friction fire.

Warnings/Comments

Some people report minor throat irritation when consuming the plant, even when cooked; sample a small taste and wait a bit to check your body's reaction. The Ozarks is home to around 22 species of *Oenothera*; several are planted ornamentally. The pink-flowering *O. speciosa* (showy evening primrose) is common on roadsides. *O. missouriensis* (Missouri evening primrose) is a low-growing glade resident with large yellow flowers. *O. biennis* has been naturalized in temperate climates around the world and is commercially cultivated to make medicinally beneficial evening primrose oil.

OXALIDACEAE (SORRELS)

This small family of trees, shrubs, and herbaceous plants consists of 570 species in 5 genera. Most species are herbaceous with 5-petaled flowers and have divided leaves that exhibit "sleep movement," closing at night. The genus *Averrhoa* contains the tree species that produces star fruit.

VIOLET AND YELLOW WOOD SORREL
(AKA SOURGRASS, WILD SHAMROCK, SHEEP SHOWERS)
Oxalis violacea, O. stricta

Native

Edible: leaves, flowers, seeds

An early memory of wild plants was learning about "sheep showers" from my mother. My childhood rambles to nearby Pearson Creek always included snagging a few handfuls of the tart leaves and seed pod "pickles" to eat along the way.

Yellow wood sorrel

Description
Violet wood sorrel (*O. violacea*) is a low-growing perennial that emerges from bulbs, with flowers that are typically taller than the leaves. Leaves are trifoliate, up to 1" across, in clusters on single stalks up to 6". Heart-shaped leaflets are dark green, with dark purple markings and purple undersides. The 5-petaled flowers are lavender to pale magenta, ¼"–½" across, on umbels at the top of stalks up to 8" tall. The flowers mature to small, inconspicuous egg-shaped fruits. *O. stricta* and other yellow-flowering *Oxalis* species will form erect, many-branched and often hairy, weak stems up to 15" tall. Leaves are similar to *O. violacea*, but are light green and often larger. Flowers occur in small umbels at the leaf axil. Fruits (pickles) are upright, elongated capsules containing tiny black seeds. The capsules can expel the seeds a short distance when touched.

Habitat/Range
O. violacea is found in partially to mostly shaded areas, rocky open woodlands, glades, prairies, and wooded roadsides, mostly in acid soils. *O. stricta* is widespread and tolerant of a wide range of conditions, occurring in open fields and edges, urban lawns and lots, waste areas, gardens, and other disturbed ground areas. Both species range throughout most of North America. Absent from a few western states.

Uses
Raw leaves and seeds make a good trail nibble or a tasty addition to salads or sandwiches. When paired with peppergrass (*Lepidium* spp.), it adds a nice lemon-pepper flavor to any dish. Can be added to soups or other cooked dishes to add flavor or steeped to make a tart beverage.

Warnings/Comments

The tart flavor comes from oxalic acid. All plants containing high levels can cause stomach distress and other conditions if consumed in excess. The houseplant shamrock (*Oxalis triangularis*), a South American relative of wood sorrel, has the same characteristic flavor of the genus.

RECIPE

Creamed Wood Sorrel Soup

3 tablespoons butter

½ cup finely chopped wild onion or shallots

6 packed cups chopped violet or yellow wood sorrel leaves

4½ cups vegetable stock or seasoned water from boiled greens

½ cup Marsala wine

½ cup heavy cream

Salt

1. Melt butter in a stockpot. Add onions and sauté till tender; add the vegetable stock and wine. Turn the heat to medium.

2. Stir in the sorrel leaves, and cook a couple minutes till the leaves are wilted. Reduce heat, cover, and cook another 10 minutes, stirring occasionally.

3. Whisk in the cream; salt to taste and let simmer on very low heat for about 5 minutes.

4. Serve garnished with chopped wild onion tops and fresh sorrel leaves and flowers.

PASSIFLORACEAE (PASSIONFLOWERS)

Passiflora consists of a single genus with about 550 species; many are tropical in origin. Most are vines; several are woody shrubs or trees. Many species produce showy, complex flowers and thick-skinned fruits that contain multiple seeds. The seeds are surrounded by fleshy sacs called arils.

PURPLE PASSIONFLOWER (AKA MAYPOP)
Passiflora incarnata

Native

Edible: fruits, buds, flowers, leaves, seeds

Passionflower fruit, with arils and seeds

I discovered this distinctive native plant as a kid after stepping on something in the grass that made a loud pop. It had a sweet smell when I picked it up, so I had to taste it. (Kids, right?) I liked the sweet, slightly citrusy flavor but was afraid to eat much till I knew what they were. I was happy to learn that other people ate "maypops." Nowadays, any fall drive on an Ozarks backroad involves scanning open fencerows to spot the ripe fruits.

Description

A fast-growing, perennial climbing or trailing vine with many axillary tendrils. Alternate leaves are 2½"–5½" long, each with 3 to occasionally 5 deeply palmate lobes and finely serrated margins. The elaborate, showy flowers appear in June–September, forming singly on stalks arising from leaf axils. Each flower consists of a 3"-wide radiating corona of fine, lavender or purple threadlike wavy appendages atop 10 pale lavender to light purple tepals. The reproductive system consists of 5 yellowish anthers, 3 green styles, and a green ovary on a short stem in the center of the inflorescence. Egg-shaped, green-husked fruits up to 3" long form on the flower stems, eventually becoming brown and wrinkled. Inside the husks are numerous sweet arils, each containing a round and flattened black seed.

Passionflower arils and seeds

Habitat/Range
Found in un-mowed pastures, old fields, prairies, streambanks, thickets, disturbed open areas, fencerows, and along roadsides and railroads. Range is throughout most of the lower midwestern and southeastern United States, north to Kansas and Pennsylvania, south to Texas and Florida.

Uses
The glob of fragrant, sweet arils inside the ripe fruits are a great trail nibble; you can strain off the sweet flesh in your mouth and spit out the seeds or just crunch down the whole works. The juice makes an exquisite jelly or syrup; it is also good for wine. Cook the arils in a bit of water till the flesh is separating from the seeds, then push through a wire strainer over a bowl to collect the juice. Flowers are edible raw and make a beautiful addition to salads. Husks of younger fruits can be boiled as a vegetable. Leaves are commonly used as a mild sedative tea used to treat a number of conditions, such as insomnia, anxiety, muscle spasms, and ADHD, and as an aid in opiate withdrawal.

Warnings/Comments
Many commercial cultivars are available for flower gardens. Fruit is grown and used commercially for a food flavoring. The green plant is a larval host for several butterfly species.

PHYTOLACCACEAE (POKEWEEDS)

This family's taxonomic status is still under debate; different sources report a range from 33 species in 5 genera to 65 species in 18 genera. Most are trees, shrubs, and herbaceous plants with tropical or subtropical origins; several are found in temperate climates. Many have common characteristics, such as simple leaves with entire margins and fleshy, racemose fruits.

POKEWEED (AKA POKE SALLET)
Phytolacca americana

Native

Edible: boiled shoots, boiled young leaves, berry juice

My first memory of foraging was collecting pokeweed with my mom. She served it like all boiled greens—with bacon grease, salt, and vinegar. Many avoid it because of misinformation and miss out on one of the tastiest cooked greens when they are carefully harvested and prepared. It is also called "poke salad," but the actual term is "sallet," which refers to cooked greens. You certainly wouldn't use it raw in a salad. (See Uses and Warnings.)

Description

A large, pithy-hollow branching stem to 10' tall with smooth, pale green skin, maturing to bright purple. Alternate, light green leaves are lanceolate to ovate, up to 10" long and 4" wide, with smooth margins and prominent veins on ½"–1" petioles. Small white flowers form in cylindrical clusters on 3"–6" terminal racemes and mature to drooping clusters of dark purple, juicy berries. Each is about ¼" across, containing 10 small, oval black seeds.

Habitat/Range

This native, disturbed-ground colonizer can be found in barn lots, pastures, old fields, damp meadows, edges of bottom-lands and moist forested slopes, fence-rows, power line cuts, roadsides, bases and ledges of bluffs, streambanks, and pond and lake edges. Range is through-out the eastern United States and Canada. Mostly absent from the Dakotas to Idaho and from Nevada to Colorado.

Uses

The entire plant is considered toxic, but early shoots up to 8" tall and tender tops of young plants under a foot tall are con-sidered the most delicious of potherbs after boiling to remove toxins. Many sources advise boiling in three waters. In my experience, small shoots and young

Pokeberries

leaves only require a single long boil, till the water turns greenish. On plants up to a cou-ple feet tall, take only the tender topmost leaves and stem, and boil in two waters. Seeds are toxic, but the berry juice can be used for jelly and wine after straining out seeds. The juice also makes a good purple dye. Cherokee and other indigenous tribes used a specific dosage of dried seeds to relieve arthritis pain. The roots were used medicinally, but any medicine made from toxic plants is all about dosage—a mistake could be fatal.

Warnings/Comments

In early foraging experiments, I once tried steaming the leaves instead of boiling. The results were probably akin to eating a box of Ex-Lax, resulting in cramps and explosive diarrhea. Lesson learned. The toxin levels increase as the plant gets larger, so avoid collect-ing when the stalks start turning purple. When harvesting shoots, take care to avoid any pieces of taproot. When trying pokeweed for the first time, boil well in at least two waters, and eat only a small quantity to check your body's reaction. The toxic berries are attractive to toddlers, and consumption of even a few berries could be fatal.

PLANTAGINACEAE (PLANTAINS)

Due to recent upheavals in classification, this herbaceous family is now considered to include about 1,900 species in 94 genera worldwide in various structural forms. Fifty-two genera are represented in the United States, and the genus *Penstemon* accounts for more than half of the 247 species. All are herbs with predominantly undivided basal leaves and flowers produced in elongated or branched clusters. Most species have flowers with 4 sepals that are fused at the base and a 2-lipped corolla, with the lower lip divided into 3 lobes and the upper lip into 2.

BROAD-LEAVED PLANTAIN
(AKA COMMON PLANTAIN, WHITE MAN'S FOOT)
Plantago major

Introduced

Edible: leaves, shoots, seeds

Description

This well-known European invader forms a basal rosette with large, oval, shiny and leathery leaves up to 12" long, each with 5–9 prominent lateral veins and smooth margins, tapering to a long petiole. When broken, the petiole contains stringlike threads that continue into the leaf veins. Flower spikes grow up to 15" from the base, forming inconspicuous flowers on the upper two-thirds of their length that mature to densely packed fruit capsules, each containing 6–20 brown seeds. Narrow-leaved plantain (*Plantago lanceolata*) has narrower, less fleshy, lanceolate leaves with a cone-shaped flower atop a long, naked stalk. The Ozarks is also home to native plantain species such as heart-leaved (*P. cordata*), dwarf (*P. virginica*), bracted (*P. aristata*), and blackseed (*P. rugelii*).

Habitat/Range

Found throughout the United States and southern Canada in moist, disturbed ground and open areas, especially lawns, fields, urban/suburban waste areas, and roadsides nearer to human habitation. Tolerates a high degree of disturbances like trampling and mowing. Native to Europe and Asia; naturalized in many other countries around the globe.

Uses

Raw shoots and young leaves are a highly nutritious addition to salads or can be blanched or sautéed to improve flavor. Before they become tough and fibrous, larger leaves can be used in soups or boiled with other greens as a potherb. Seeds can be consumed raw, boiled like rice, or dried and ground for use as a flour additive or in seedcakes. Has extensive medicinal uses; most commonly used raw as a poultice or made into an ointment to treat wounds, stings, rashes, and other skin ailments. Tea from the leaves is used to treat bronchitis, colds, sinus infections, and stomach ulcers.

Warnings/Comments

Plantain has caused contact dermatitis in some. It can cause diarrhea and a blood-pressure drop when eaten in excess, although reports of either are very rare. It is one of the most widely distributed and commonly used edible/medicinal plants in the world. Scientific studies confirm that broad-leaved plantain is vitamin rich and contains bioactive compounds and antimicrobial properties for use in treating a number of ailments and conditions. Not related to *Musa* spp. (cultivated cooking bananas), also called plantains.

POLYGONACEAE (BUCKWHEATS, KNOTWEEDS, SMARTWEEDS)

This weedy family includes rhubarb and buckwheat and contains about 1,200 species distributed into about 48 genera. *Polygonum* is derived from ancient Greek. "Poly" (many) and "gonum" (joints or knees) refers to the characteristic swollen nodes on the stems of many species.

CLIMBING FALSE BUCKWHEAT
(AKA CRESTED BUCKWHEAT, INDIAN WHEAT)
Fallopia scandens

Native

Edible: leaves, stems, flowers, seeds

Description

An aggressive, climbing vine, this perennial can form large, twining mats on trees, shrubs, and structures. Stems are round, have swollen nodes with an attached membranous sheath at the leaf axils, and are light green to red and up to 20' long. Alternate leaves are ovate to heart shaped, up to 6" long and 3" wide, with smooth margins. Lower leaves are on long petioles; upper leaves are nearly sessile. Blooms appear July–November; large clusters of yellow-green to pinkish, minute flowers form on racemes at leaf axils along stems. Flower is a 5-parted calyx with 3 outer tepals that are strongly winged. Three-angled, winged fruits (similar to buckwheat) approximately ⅓" long will mature to contain smooth, shiny, brownish to black tri-cornered seeds.

Climbing false buckwheat seeds

Habitat/Range

Found in moist, mostly open areas in bottoms, valleys, glades, streambanks, edges of impounded waters, sloughs, and seeps, ledges and tops of bluffs, croplands, fencerows, ditches, railroads, and roadsides. Ranges throughout eastern North America and Canada, west to Texas, Colorado, and Wyoming.

Uses

Tender young leaves and stems can be eaten raw as a salad green, cooked as a potherb, added to other cooked dishes, or blended with sweetened water for a tart drink. Older stems can be cut up and used like rhubarb. Seeds can be eaten raw, dried for use in seed-cakes, or ground with other seeds as a flour substitute.

Warnings/Comments

Toxic look-alikes in the genus *Convulvus* (bindweeds related to morning glory) have large, trumpet-like flowers and milky sap and lack the swollen nodes with membranous sheaths (ocrea). Like most in the family Polygonaceae, the tart acidic taste is due to oxalic acid. Those prone to kidney stones or gout should avoid it. The genus *Fallopia* has a complicated taxonomic history and was recently split from *Polygonum*. *F. convulvus* (black bindweed) is a similar European invasive considered to be an agricultural pest. It usually develops shorter vines than *F. scandens*, and its seeds lack papery wings and are dull instead of shiny.

Pink smartweed   White smartweed

SMARTWEEDS
(LADIES' THUMB, DOTTED SMARTWEED, JUMPSEED)
Persicaria spp.

Introduced, with similar natives

Edible: shoots, leaves, flower heads

Description

An erect-stemmed perennial found in dense colonies, usually in moist or disturbed ground. Stems are slightly zigzagged, with swollen nodes at the bends at leaf axils. Alternate leaves are on short petioles or sessile, mostly lanceolate, with smooth margins and sharp tips, up to 5" long but usually smaller. Spikelike cylindrical flower clusters up to 1½" long occur at the tips of stems. Individual flowers are pink, up to ⅛" across. *P. amphibia* is usually larger and has an aquatic form appearing quite different from the terrestrial form, usually hairless when growing in water. Terrestrial forms often have hairy stems or leaves. *P. punctatum* (water pepper, dotted smartweed) is similar but with white flowers. *P.*

virginiana (jumpseed) has larger, broader leaves and a flower spike up to 16" with sparse, small white flowers. The oval, pod-like dried seeds will jump off the stem when touched. There are at least 30+ species of *Persicaria* in the Ozarks, all with similar characteristics.

Jumpseed young leaves

Habitat/Range

Found in swamps, seeps, wet ditches, gravel bars, streambanks, and borders of lakes, ponds, and sloughs. Many species can live submerged in water or soggy ground. *P. maculosa* is a European species, introduced throughout the United States and Canada; other species mentioned are native.

Uses

The young tender leaves and pink flower heads have a mild flavor and are a good addition to green salads. Young shoots can be boiled as a potherb or added to cooked dishes such as stir-fries, soups, and quiche. Most species with white flowers have a very peppery flavor (except for the mild-flavored *P. virginianum*) and are best used sparingly or can be dried and used as a seasoning. If you're unsure as to species within the genus, chew a leaf to taste-test; some get unpleasantly peppery after a bit.

Warnings/Comments

A European nickname for this peppery-tasting plant is "arse-smart," as some species, such as *P. hydropiper* (water pepper), contain high levels of peppery oils that can cause skin irritation and can apparently survive the digestive tract and cause problems when they leave the body after consumption. This species is cultivated to a milder form in Japan for culinary purposes. *Reynoutria japonica*

Japanese knotweed

(Japanese knotweed) is a fairly new aggressive invader, up to 8' tall, with large ovate to heart-shaped leaves. Leaves are edible, but take great caution to avoid spreading seeds, as it has become a major pest in many areas.

FIELD SORREL
(AKA SOUR DOCK, RED SORREL, SHEEP SORREL)
Rumex acetosella

Introduced

Edible: leaves, shoots, flowers, seeds

Description

A low-growing herbaceous perennial that first emerges as a basal rosette up to 6" across, with a slender, erect flowering stalk up to 1' tall, but usually shorter. Spreads by rhizomes and often forms colonies. Basal leaves are up to 3" long and 1" across, spear shaped and narrowing at the base, with 2 spreading basal lobes. Blade surface is smooth, with smooth margins. Tiny brownish-red flowers form in racemes on branched, green to reddish flower stalks.

Habitat/Range

Prefers mostly open or disturbed ground habitats. Found in gardens, lawns, pastures, old fields, glades, prairies, and along paths and roadsides. Native to Europe; range is throughout North America and Canada.

Uses

Vitamin-packed, nutrient-dense, and loaded with healthful phenolic compounds, the leaves and young stems

Field sorrel flowers

are great as a lemony-tasting trail nibble or tart addition to raw salads. Can be used in sauces, soups, and other cooked dishes when a sour or tart element is desired. Can be dried and ground into flour as a thickener or used to make noodles. Seeds can be eaten raw or cooked. Used medicinally as a diuretic and for other ailments; used topically for its astringent properties.

Warnings/Comments

As with all plants containing high amounts of oxalates, consume only small quantities when raw to avoid stomach distress. Avoid entirely if you're prone to kidney stones or related ailments. Cooking reduces oxalate levels to negligible amounts.

CURLY DOCK (AKA YELLOW DOCK)
Rumex crispus

Introduced

Edible: leaves, shoots, stalks, seeds

This highly nutritious potherb was another of my mom's favorite wild greens, usually boiled with pokeweed and served with the ever-present bacon grease and vinegar. I was an adult before I knew boiled greens and most cooked vegetables had a flavor other than bacon.

Description

This common herbaceous perennial starts from a taproot. First-year growth is a small basal rosette of dark green oval to lanceolate leaves that mature to 6" long and 1" across with pointed ends. Young leaves have smooth margins, becoming crisped and wavy with age. A distinguishing feature is the papery sheath (ocrea) that forms on the leaf stem as it emerges from the root or stalk. Second-year plants form a ridged flower stalk up to 4', with alternate leaves along the stalk, usually branching as it flowers. Clusters of green flowers appears on panicles of racemes at the ends of stems and branches, maturing to reddish-brown clusters of papery-husked, 3-angled brown seeds. The dried flower stalks and seed clusters often persist into winter.

Habitat/Range
Found in open, disturbed ground in a range of soil conditions. Common in pastures, old fields, glades, garden edges, roadsides, degraded wetlands, cultivated fields, and waste areas. Native to Eurasia; range is throughout the United States and Canada.

Curly dock

Uses

Young, tender leaves and shoots can be used raw sparingly in salads. Older leaves and peeled stalks are boiled as a potherb or used in soups, but harvest while they still have a slight mucilaginous texture; dry leaves are usually tough. Tender stems can be pickled. Leaves and shoots can be blanched or sautéed and frozen for later use. Seeds can be winnowed, ground, and used as a flour additive, or ground with other seeds such as lamb's quarter and climbing false buckwheat mixed with wheat flour to make tasty crackers. For quick relief of temporary itching from contact with stinging or wood nettles, crush a few moist leaves of dock or jewelweed (*Impatiens capensis*) and scrub the affected area.

Warnings/Comments

Contains fairly high amounts of oxalic acid and calcium oxalates; consuming large quantities can result in stomach distress. People with liver or kidney dysfunction, kidney stones, or rheumatoid arthritis should avoid plants high in oxalic acid.

RECIPE

Curly Dock Nori

4 cups chopped curly dock leaves (or mix with lamb's quarter or any flavorful seasonal greens)

5 cloves garlic

1 tablespoon chopped peppergrass tops

White smartweed leaves (or 1 teaspoon black pepper)

1 teaspoon soy sauce

1 teaspoon water

1. Blend all ingredients to a paste in a food processor or blender. Add water if needed; the mixture should be thick like tomato paste.

2. Lay parchment paper on a flat baking pan. Spread paste in a thin layer on the parchment paper; dehydrate at 125°F for about 12 hours, or until crunchy. (**Note:** To speed things up, bake in the oven at 200°F till the mixture starts to dry a bit; flip mixture and turn off the oven to prevent burning.)

3. Use the nori as you would chips, or crumble over the top of soups and other dishes.

PORTULACEAE (PURSLANES)

This family is mostly fleshy-leaved herbaceous plants or shrubs in a single genus consisting of about 115 species. The highest diversity occurs in semiarid regions of the Southern Hemisphere in Africa, Australia, and South America. A few species extend north into temperate and arctic regions.

SPRING BEAUTY (AKA FAIRY SPUD)
Claytonia virginica

Native

Edible: leaves, flowers, tubers
This beautiful perennial has delicate, pink-striped white flowers and can be found in blooming carpets with other early-spring ephemerals. Any plant that produces something called "fairy spuds" is a winner in my book.

Description
One to several narrow, lanceolate leaves 2"–5" long emerge from a corm, dark green to purplish in color. The weak flowering stem usually has 1 or 2 sets of opposite leaves, terminating in a raceme of 3–6 flowers. Flowers are up to ½" wide, each with 5 white, pink-striped petals and 5 central stamens with pink anthers. Root is a round white corm with a brown skin and attached rootlets up to ½".

Habitat/Range

Widespread throughout the Ozarks in a number of habitats; found in open woodlands, hollows, bottoms, rocky ledges, and in urban lawns. Range is throughout mid to eastern North America, west to Texas and Nebraska, north into Canada. Mostly absent from Florida and northern New England states.

Uses

All aerial parts are a nice addition to salad greens; the leaves have a slight citrus-sweet flavor. The flowers add a nice bit of color and sweetness. The root can be eaten raw or cooked and used as you would potatoes. Flavor is similar to potato but a bit sweeter.

Warnings/Comments

As with all natives, only collect roots when found in large colonies. The root corm can be harvested any time, but is best when collected in late winter or early spring as the leaves are forming. Be on the lookout for similar but larger corms possibly present in the colony, which could be jack-in-the-pulpit corms (*Arisaema triphyllum*). During our early foraging adventures, Don Brink and I made the mistake of relying on a less-than-accurate booklet on wild edibles. It stated that Native Americans ate the cooked root corm of *A. triphyllum*, but it had a hot, peppery taste when eaten raw. We both like peppery flavors, so we tried it. The book didn't mention that the origin of the "peppery" taste was calcium oxalate crystals—it felt like we both had mouthfuls of finely-ground glass for the rest of the evening! Lesson learned.

PURSLANE
Portulaca oleracea

Introduced

Edible: leaves, stems, seeds
Purslane is currently receiving much attention in the media due to its superfood status. It has the highest levels of a type of plant-based omega-3 fatty acids and is packed with beneficial vitamins and minerals.

Description

Reddish, succulent stems radiate from a central taproot, typically prostrate and sprawling, but occasionally upright. It often forms dense mats. The thick, fleshy leaves are up to 1¼" long, spatulate, smooth with smooth margins, alternate or opposite, clustered at stem joints and ends. Small yellow, 5-petaled flowers form singly on leaf axils, maturing to form small seedpods containing numerous tiny, black seeds.

Habitat/Range

This disturbed-ground invader tolerates a wide variety of soil conditions and is drought-tolerant. Found in open habitats such as barnyards, gardens, croplands, rocky bluffs, gravel roadsides, abandoned urban lots, and cracks in sidewalks. Its original range possibly India and Persia, it is now found nearly worldwide due to anthropogenic distribution.

Uses

Leaves and stems are used raw in salads and make a nice addition to just about any raw or cooked dish. The taste is a citrusy tang with a slight pepper finish and goes well with nearly anything. Its slightly mucilaginous quality makes it a good addition to soups and stir-fries and also makes a great base for pesto. The tart taste is due to malic and oxalic acids. As with many plants growing in desert or dry environments, it has more flavor when harvested in the morning. The seeds can be added to other ground seeds and ingredients to make nutritious seedcakes.

Warnings/Comments

Common in vacant city lots, sidewalks, or other places where harvest might not be advisable. Fortunately, they are easily transplanted or grown from seed. Not typically found in pristine habitats. Purslane is increasingly available in farmers' markets and health food stores due to its nice flavor and numerous health benefits. It has long been considered to be of European origin, but recent archaeological evidence shows that it was used by indigenous peoples in pre-Columbian North America. This appears to be a mystery. Was it already here, or did Vikings bring it?

RECIPE

Wild Pesto

3 cups fresh mixed greens

4–5 bulbs wild onion (or 4–6 cloves garlic)

¼–½ cup seeds or nuts

¼ cup extra virgin olive oil

½ cup freshly grated Parmesan

Splash of lemon juice or small bunch of wood sorrel leaves

Salt and pepper to taste

Crush ingredients together in a *molcajete* or put in a food processor. Add olive oil a bit at a time to preferred viscosity; add salt and pepper to taste.

I like to use a mix of both mild and sharp flavors. Mild flavors can be anything with moist or fleshy leaves, such as purslane, lamb's quarter, henbit/dead nettle, violet leaves, chickweed, pink smartweed, etc. Plants with sharper flavors include dittany, horseweed, wild bergamot or other mints, spicebush, white smartweed, peppergrass, and watercress.

ROSACEAE (ROSES, APPLES, NUMEROUS FRUITS AND BERRIES)

This family of herbs, shrubs, and trees consists of about 4,828 known species in 91 genera. It contains many important food species, such as apples, pears, plums, cherries, apricots, almonds, blackberries, strawberries, and ornamental shrubs such as roses and hawthorns.

DOWNY SERVICEBERRY
(AKA SARVUS, SHADBUSH, JUNEBERRY)
Amelanchier arborea

Native

Edible: flowers, berries

At the end of winter, the appearance of serviceberry's snow-white blooms on our leafless forested slopes is often a first indicator of spring, serving as a reminder to get out and search for early edibles! It's also our earliest-ripening native berry.

Description

A multistemmed shrub or tree up to 35' tall. Young limbs have smooth, often mottled gray bark that becomes ridged and furrowed with age, especially at the base of larger trunks. Simple, light green leaves are 2"–5" long, alternate, oval with a pointed tip, with finely serrated margins. Young shoots and leaves are covered in downy hair, becoming less so as they mature. Blooms appear in early or mid-March–late April, before the foliage appears. Flowers have 5 wavy, long and narrow white petals that are slightly spaced, forming on 4"–7" racemes at the tips of shoots in drooping clusters of 6–14 flowers. Flowering racemes mature in mid-June, forming clusters of fruits. Individual berries are round, ¼"–½", ripening to dark red or purple.

Habitat/Range

Found in open, mature woodlands, rocky slopes, limestone glades, above bluffs, and along streambanks. Occurs throughout the Ozarks and the southeastern United States. Absent from the lower Mississippi Valley, Florida, and coastal areas north to Virginia. Numerous species of *Amelanchier* occur over much of the United States and Canada.

Uses

Great for cereal or dessert toppings, or add to muffins, pancakes, bread, soups, etc. Makes excellent jam and wine. Dried serviceberries were a preferred addition to pemmican, a dried meat-and-berry travel food used by indigenous tribes. One preparation method uses a skinned and eviscerated rabbit or squirrel carcass that is dried whole then pounded to a fine mush and mixed with rendered fat and a handful of dried berries. This can be stuffed into a length of smoked deer intestine, much like a sausage. The rendered fat acted as a preservative; the sought-after fatty marrow inside the pulverized bones was retained, and the dried berries provided vitamin C to make it a complete food.

Warnings/Comments

Commonly planted as an attractive ornamental shrub, with several cultivars available. The berries attract wildlife, and leaves are very colorful in the fall. The blooms are an important nectar source for early-emerging pollinators.

DOWNY HAWTHORN
Crataegus mollis

Native

Edible: flowers, leaves, buds, berries

Hawthorn is the state flower of Missouri, but lawmakers who wrote the law designated no individual species of *Crataegus*. Among the possible 75 species that occur in the state, *C. mollis* is quite common, and the Missouri Department of Conservation considers it to be the species lawmakers intended to enshrine with its designation.

Description

A shrub or small tree with single or multiple trunks and crooked branches; often forms a rounded crown. Trunk bark is gray-brown and shallowly furrowed with scaly plates. Branches are gray and generally smooth with sparse, woody spines. Twig bark is brownish with white lenticels. Alternate, simple leaves are 3"–5" long and 2"–4" across, forming on hairy petioles that emerge from twigs and shoots. Leaf blades are variably oval, spatulate, or triangulate, with pointed or serrated lobes along the margins. Blooms April–June, with clusters of white flowers forming on twig spurs. Individual flowers are up to 1" across, each having 5 petals and numerous yellow stamens. Fertile flowers are replaced by ½"-long reddish fruits resembling crabapples, each containing numerous small seeds.

Habitat/Range

Found in a variety of habitats, often in rocky conditions on hillsides, streambanks, woodlands and borders, thickets, savannas, and abandoned pastures. Some species are more often associated with bottomlands. Range is the eastern and midwestern United States and Canada, west to Texas and North Dakota, east to Pennsylvania and Virginia. Absent from most southern Atlantic coastal states.

Uses

Remove seeds before consuming. Process by cooking ripe fruits, then harvest pulp by squeezing through cheesecloth or fine screen to remove seeds. The pulp can be used for or added to jellies, sauces, syrups, and wines and other beverages. Perfectly ripe fruits contain a high amount of pectin; pulp can be added to other fruit jellies when commercial pectin isn't available. Tender young leaves, flower buds, and flowers can be eaten as a trail nibble or added to salads. Hawthorn is known for its health benefits and was used for centuries by ancient Druids, Greek and Chinese herbalists, and other cultures. It is commercially available as a supplement.

Warnings/Comments

The seeds contain the toxin amygdalin, an almond-scented hydrogen cyanide precursor found in the seeds of apples and many other related fruits. It can be harmful when metabolized during consumption after the seeds are crushed or chewed. *Malus* spp. (crabapples) have similar fruits, leaves, growth, and flowering structure; some varieties are too tart or bitter for consumption.

WILD STRAWBERRY
Fragaria virginiana

Native

Edible: berries, leaves
Encountering a large patch of ripe wild strawberries is the ultimate in flavorful foraging. Just remember to leave a few for the box turtles and other critters!

Description

A low-growing herbaceous perennial up to 6" tall, spreading by horizontal runners. Trifoliate basal leaves are on long, hairy stems. Each leaflet is ovate to obovate, up to 2½" long and 1½" wide, with toothed margins and hairy undersides. Blooms April–May, with umbel-like clusters of 4–6

flowers on long, hairy stalks. Flowers are up to ¾" across, with 5 rounded white petals and many central yellow stamens. Fertile flowers mature in June–July to red, fleshy strawberries up to ½" across, with tiny seeds in sunken pits across the entire surface. Technically, it is an aggregate fruit, not a berry. *Duchesnea indica* (Indian or mock strawberry) is a similar, weedy nonnative with yellow flowers instead of white. The berries are white-fleshed and tasteless, but nutritious.

Habitat/Range

Found in open woodlands and their borders, prairies, old fields, glades, rocky hillsides, savannas, and along roadsides. Tolerates a wide range of open and partly shaded conditions; occurs in disturbed or pristine habitats. Ranges throughout the continental United States and Canada.

Uses

Great as a trail nibble. If you're lucky enough to find a large patch, collect and use as you would any berry, or use your imagination to concoct yet-unheard-of goodies. Best used fresh; the flavor is superior to the larger domesticated varieties. Green or fully dried leaves make good tea. The leaves and fruit are used medicinally to treat a number of ailments.

Warnings/Comments

Our common domesticated strawberry was first cultivated in eighteenth-century France and is a hybrid between *F. virginiana* and *F. chiloensis*, a South American species.

WILD PLUM (AKA AMERICAN PLUM)
Prunus americanus

Native

Edible: fruits

Description

A multistemmed, thicket-forming shrub or small tree to 20' tall. Trunk can be up to 12" diameter, with rough, gray to reddish-brown bark. Smaller stems are mostly smooth with lateral lenticels. Growth pattern of thicket stems can be twiggy and contorted, often with short spines. Alternate, simple leaves are ovate to obovate, 2½"–4" long, 1½"–2" wide, with pale undersides and sharply serrated margins. Blooms appear April–May before foliage is present, forming at leaf axils in clusters of 2–5 flowers. Each flower is on a short stalk with 5 white petals, 5 greenish sepals, and numerous stamens, up to 1" across. Fertilized flowers mature into globe-shaped yellow to red fruits up to 1" across, with juicy, sweet or tart flesh when fully ripe (July–September). Each fruit contains a round and slightly flattened pit.

Wild plums

Habitat/Range

Found in glades, savannas, thickets, fencerows, abandoned pastures, ravines, streambanks, roadsides, power line cuts, and open mesic woodlands and their borders. Can colonize disturbed, open ground, but is often shaded out by larger canopy species. Range is throughout most of the United States and eastern Canada. Absent from Texas, Nevada, California, Oregon, and Idaho.

Uses

Great as a trail nibble but makes the best jam or jelly ever slapped on a biscuit. Also good for pies, fruit salads, fruit leather, wine, brandy, sauces, or syrup, and can be dried or frozen for later use. Flavor varies widely among individual plants, from sweet to extremely tart.

Warnings/Comments

Leaves, twigs, and pits of most species in the genus *Prunus* (cherries, peaches, and plums) contain the compound amygdaline, which breaks down into hydrogen cyanide when ingested. Wild plum is the source for numerous cultivar species that are sold commercially. *P. angustifolia* (Chickasaw plum) is similar, but with narrower leaves and a generally southern range; it is more commonly found in Arkansas and eastern Oklahoma.

WILD BLACK CHERRY
Prunus serotina

Native

Edible: fruits

Description
A straight-trunked tree up to 60' or taller, with a narrow, rounded crown and simple leaves. Bark is reddish-brown and smooth, with raised white, horizontal lenticels on saplings and branches. Trunk bark on older trees is darker and rough, with the surface broken into small plates with upturned edges. Twigs are reddish brown, slender and smooth, with a bitter-almond smell when broken. Alternate, leathery leaves up to 6" long and 2" wide emerge on branches and twigs. They form on petioles up to 1", are ovate to lanceolate-ovate, with pointed tips and a rounded base. Upper leaf surface is dark green and shiny; undersides are pale with hairs on the midvein. Margins are finely serrated. Blooms April–May, with drooping, cylindrical racemes of white flowers up to 6" long and 2" across, forming on twigs and leafy branches. Flowers are 5-petaled, tightly clustered, and radially symmetrical. In August–October, raceme stems become red, and flowers are replaced by shiny black globoid fruits approximately ¼" across, each containing a single, round pit.

Habitat/Range
Found in open, oak-hickory woodlands and borders, savannas, glades, roadsides, fence-rows, power line cuts, and streambanks; prefers rich soil and open habitats. Range is mostly the eastern and midwestern United states and eastern Canada. Also occurs in Arizona, New Mexico, Washington, and British Columbia.

Uses
The tart berries are great for jams, syrups, sauces, wines, and cordials. Flavor varies among individual trees. Some are sweet enough to eat raw; others are overly tart and are improved by cooking with sugar or other sweetener. Pitting individual raw fruits can be time-consuming but worth it when you find a sweet batch. Process by cooking and mashing, then remove the seeds. The bark is used medicinally for bronchial and throat irritation; it's not toxic in small doses.

Warnings/Comments
The seeds, leaves, and twigs of plants in this genus contain alkaloids that break down into toxic cyanide compounds, thus the bitter-almond taste and smell. This plant is possibly responsible for the highest number of livestock poisonings of any eastern plant; the effect is exacerbated in wilted leaves.

BLACKBERRY, DEWBERRY, BLACK RASPBERRY
Rubus allegheniensis, R. flagellaris, R. occidentalis

Native

Edible: fruits, flowers

Many Ozarkians engage in the midsummer ritual of berry picking. It's always worth battling ticks, chiggers, and brambles in the heat of late June and early July when heavenly cobbler and pie are the end result. Despite the name, these are aggregate fruits, not true berries.

Description

R. allegheniensis is an erect, spreading bramble with arching canes up to 8' tall. First-year canes and new growth on older canes are green and prickly, becoming ridged and brown with numerous decurved thorns with age. Compound, alternate leaves have 3–5 leaflets on long petioles; the end leaflet is typically larger. Leaflets are up to 5" long and 3" wide, ovate, with coarsely toothed margins; their undersurface is usually paler and slightly pubescent. Flowers form on racemes longer than they are wide, blooming April–June. Each raceme typically has 10–20 flowers, each with 5 oval white petals, 5 pointed sepals, and numerous stamens. Shiny, purplish-black aggregate fruits are around ¾" long, globe-shaped to cylindrical, appearing in late June–August. *R. occidentalis* (black raspberry) has round, green to purplish arching canes with a whitish coating and has smaller straight thorns. Compound leaves tend to be trifoliate, with white undersides. The soft fruit is easily removed, leaving the torus on the stem and a thimble-like depression in the fruit. *R. flagellaris* is similar to blackberry, but with shorter, low-trailing vines, smaller leaves, larger flowers, and larger fruits that ripen earlier.

Habitat/Range
Found in woodland borders, valleys, fencerows, abandoned pastures, glades, savannas, old fields, thickets, and along roadsides. Range is the eastern United States and Canada, west to Oklahoma and Nebraska; introduced to California and British Columbia. Absent from most Gulf Coast states.

Black raspberry

Uses
Eat on the spot, or collect for use in pies, cobblers, jams, syrups, wine, brandy, or topping for any dessert or confection. Can be dried and used in pemmican and trail mix. The leaves make a nice tea and can be used in higher doses as treatment for diarrhea. Flower petals can be added to salads or drinks. The leaves and fruit have numerous health benefits and are used medicinally to treat a number of ailments.

Warnings/Comments
There are approximately 30 species of *Rubus* in the Ozarks, many of which can interbreed and hybridize. Many members of the genus are extensively cultivated around the world.

SAPINDACEAE (MAPLES, BUCKEYES)

This family of trees, woody vines, and herbaceous plants consists of about 1,858 accepted species in 138 genera, including maples, horse chestnut (buckeye), and lychee.

Silver maple samaras

SILVER MAPLE, SUGAR MAPLE, RED MAPLE—SYRUP AND SAMARAS
Acer saccharinum, A. saccharum, A. rubrum

Native

Edible: samaras, sap

Description

Silver maple is a medium to large, fast-growing tree to 100', with spreading, slender branches. Opposite, simple leaves are up to 7" long, roughly triangular, with 5 narrow, deep lobes, each with pointed tips. Upper leaf surface is pale green with a white undersurface; margins are toothed. Bark on young trees is light gray and smooth, eventually developing flat ridges and shallow furrows with age. Winged fruits (samaras) up to 2" long appear in May–June in pairs on long stalks. *A. saccharum* has a similar leaf structure, but its leaves are generally smaller and wider, with shallower lobes. *A. rubrum* is a generally smaller tree, with leaves that are occasionally 3-lobed. Both have smaller fruits than *A. saccharinum*.

Habitat/Range

A. saccharinum is found in rich moist bottomlands, streambanks, and pond margins. *A. saccharum* and *A. rubrum* are found in similar habitats; also found in upland forests, glade borders, bluff bases, and ledges. General range is throughout the eastern and midwestern United States and Canada; some species occur in a handful of western states.

Uses

Maple samaras contain a tasty bean-like fruit that is excellent raw when gathered fresh and peeled of the outer shell and wing. They can be added to salads, boiled, steamed, roasted, or dried and ground into flour. *A. saccharum* (sugar maple) has long been considered the highest producer of sap collected for syrup, but all *Acer* species and several other bottomland trees like birch, sycamore, and black walnut will produce similar sweet sap. Black walnut is the best I've tasted, producing a darker syrup with a distinct and unique flavor. Forty to 50 gallons of sap will reduce down into roughly 1 gallon of syrup; methods include slow-simmering or evaporation in large, shallow pans. Small-scale reduction can be done in any pot or pan. All methods of larger-scale reduction are best done outside because of the large volume of steam produced. The spile (spigot) for harvesting sap can be bought commercially or carved from a short length of hollow or pithy stem. The pith is cleaned out to make a hollow tube that is sharpened on one end and flat on the other. The sharp end is pounded into a small hole bored into the tree, far enough to reach the cambium layer between the wood and outer bark. A screen-covered container is tied to the tree or can be hung from the spile (if it's stout enough) to collect the sap. Sugaring season is February–early April, before leaf-out, when the sap is running highest.

Warnings/Comments

Many *Acer* species are planted ornamentally, although silver maple has soft wood and is prone to breakage in windstorms.

RECIPE

Maple Samara Mock Pistachios

Young samaras, shelled

Sea salt

Toasted sesame and/or grapeseed oil

1. Soak the young, shelled samaras for 2 days in sea salt.

2. Rinse and fry on medium heat for 3–4 minutes in oil.

3. Place samaras on paper towel to cool; dust lightly with sea salt or seasoned salt.

OHIO BUCKEYE (AKA HORSE CHESTNUT)
Aesculus glabra

Native

Edible: nuts

Folklore has it that you should carry a buckeye in your pocket for good luck. I did it often throughout my childhood, and it has worked so far; I'm still here. Despite the reputation for being toxic in their raw state, buckeyes can serve as a food source after undergoing a leaching process to remove tannins, antinutrient compounds, and toxic saponins, similar to that used with acorns.

Description

A small to medium-size tree that is often an understory species but will attain growth of up to 70' in optimal conditions. It typically has many branches that tend to droop then upturn at the ends. Young growth has brownish, smooth bark; branch and twig bark is gray and smooth. Trunk bark is gray and rough textured, becoming scaly, warty, and slightly furrowed with age. Opposite, compound leaves occur on long petioles at the ends of twigs, and have 5–7 leaflets. Individual leaflets are 3"–6" long and 1"–2" across, elliptic or elliptic-oblanceolate in shape, have serrated margins, and are nearly sessile. Blooms April–May, with flowers appearing on 4"- to 8"-long elongated, erect panicles forming at the branch tips. Individual flowers are greenish yellow, about ¾" long, with 4 petals and stamens that are longer than the petals. The distinctive fruits appear September–October as light brown, leathery capsules 1"–2¼" across; they are globe-shaped, usually with blunt spines. The husk splits into 3 parts, revealing 1 or 2, occasionally 3 shiny, brown fruits, each with a tan spot (eye) at its apex.

Habitat/Range

Found in rich soil conditions; occurring mostly in mesic to moist woodlands, valleys, ravines, river bottoms and low benches along streams, bases of slopes and bluffs, thickets, and occasionally at the edges of limestone glades. Range is mostly the eastern and mid-western United States, west to Texas and Kansas, east to the mid-Atlantic states. Absent from parts of New England and Louisiana, Florida, and South Carolina.

Uses

My limited experience with processing buckeyes involved hulling and skinning the seeds then breaking them into small bits, which were then boiled five times, each starting with new water already boiling. The leached bits were then roasted, which produced a light, crunchy cereal similar in texture to granola. See "Oaks" for leaching methods and uses for acorns; all are applicable to buckeyes. Also look for a YouTube video on processing buckeyes. A 1961 classic from the University of California's Department of Anthropology

Red buckeye nuts

shows a native woman's processing method. It involved breaking up the hulled seeds then hot-stone boiling them in twined baskets to remove skins. The mush was then placed in a leach pit, where water was poured through to remove toxins. The resulting mush was somewhat tasteless, so it was usually mixed with flavorful herbs and meat. The account below is from Dr. Daniel Moerman's book *Native American Ethnobotany*, describing this method in his account of the California's Pomo peoples' processing and use of *A. californica* (California buckeye).

"Boiled nuts were eaten with baked kelp, meat, and seafood. Nuts were put into boiling water to loosen the husk. After the husks were removed the nutmeat was returned to boiling water and cooked until it was soft like cooked potatoes. The nutmeat was then mashed with a mortar stone. The grounds could be strained at this stage or strained after soaking. The grounds would be soaked and leached a long time to remove the poisonous tannin. An older method was to peel the nuts and roast them in ashes until they were soft. They were then crushed and the meal was put in a sandy leaching basin beside a stream. For about five hours the meal was leached with water from the stream. When the bitterness disappeared it was ready to eat without further cooking."

Warnings/Comments

As noted earlier, the unprocessed seeds are toxic. When processing, continue leaching until no bitterness persists, then test with a small sample to check your body's reaction. To be safe, consume only small amounts at a time. *A. pavia* (red buckeye) is similar but has red flowers, smooth-husked fruits, usually 5 leaflets instead of 7, and has a more southern range.

SOLANACEAE (NIGHTSHADES, TOMATOES, PEPPERS, POTATOES)

This economically important family consists of about 2,700 species in 98 genera, encompassing many of our food plants, such as potatoes, tomatoes, tomatillos, eggplants, and chili peppers. Other members contain psychotropic, toxic, or medicinal alkaloids, such as *Datura* (jimsonweed), *Mandragora* (mandrake), *Atropa belladonna* (deadly nightshade), and *Nicotiana* (tobacco).

Ground cherry leaves, fruit, and flower

COMMON GROUND CHERRY (AKA HUSK TOMATO, WILD TOMATILLO)
Physalis longifolium

Native

Edible: ripe fruits

This curious-looking perennial produces sweet/tart berries covered in a papery husk and makes a delightful late-summer trail nibble. It is often difficult to locate when hiding among other plants, but it is unmistakable when the lantern-like fruits are present. More than 13 native species of *Physalis* occur in the Ozarks, all with similar characteristics.

Description

Stem is green to purplish and branched, to 2½' tall, with alternate, ovate leaves up to 5" long (usually smaller) on long petioles. Leaf margins are entire or with lobe-like, irregular teeth. Blooms May–September, with yellow, bell-shaped flowers forming singly at the leaf

Ground cherry leaves, fruit, and flower

axil. Individual flowers are about 1" across, with 5 purplish spots appearing as a ring at the base of the corolla. The flower matures into a fleshy berry about ¼" across and is encased in a drooping 1"–1½" green or purplish husk that is 5-sided with a pointed tip. The berry is green and hard at first then ripens to yellow, greenish yellow, or purple and somewhat soft.

Habitat/Range
Found in sunny to partly shaded disturbed areas, roadside ditches, pastures, cultivated fields, old fields, forest edges, savannas, ledges, open bluffs, and occasionally in bottomland and upland forest. Range is throughout the lower 48 states, north into Ontario and Quebec.

Uses
Ripe fruits are delicious raw or cooked; some describe the flavor as slightly pineapple-tomato. Add to soups or cooked dishes, use them in salsas and sweet or savory sauces, or cook them with pectin to make a great jam. To freeze fresh berries for later use, place them on a flat pan, spaced to where they don't touch. Put the pan into the freezer; when frozen, put the berries in a freezer bag to store. During one foraging class, we crushed raw ground cherries for a zesty pizza sauce on acorn-flour crust and topped it with hazelnuts, roasted wild onion, wild plums, and toasted grasshoppers.

Warnings/Comments

Use only when berries are sweet, soft, and fully ripe. Unripe berries can cause stomach irritation, and could possibly be fatal if consumed in excess. The leaves and stems of all Solanaceae are generally toxic. Some species may be somewhat bitter, but the flavor can be improved by cooking. If bitterness persists, don't consume. *Solanum americanum* (American black nightshade) is similar, but its leaves are generally more dentate and are on winged petioles. It has small white, 5-petaled flowers with yellow stamens that form on umbels, and its round, black berries are without husks. Some sources report that its fruits are toxic; others say that ripe fruits are edible. The plant apparently has varying regional levels of toxicity, so use cautiously or avoid.

Ground cherry
fruit with the husk
peeled back

RECIPE

Roasted Ground Cherry and Tomato Salsa

(adapted from Shannon Miller's award-winning recipe)

1½–2 cups ripe ground cherries, husked

2–3 small to medium yellow or Roma tomatoes, sliced

½ medium to large red onion, sliced

2 cloves garlic, chopped

1 jalapeño or other hot pepper

Olive oil

¼ cup cilantro

1 small lime, juiced

Salt to taste

1. Place tomatoes and pepper skin side up with the ground cherries, onion, and garlic in a shallow pan lined with aluminum foil; drizzle with olive oil.

2. Place in a broiler oven or grill till the skins char, making sure everything gets a little blackened.

3. Chop all roasted ingredients to moderately fine pieces, or put in a food processor and pulse several times until coarsely mixed (not soupy).

4. Put roasted ingredients in a saucepan; add the cilantro, lime, and salt to taste. Simmer 6–7 minutes.

5. Let cool before serving; best if left overnight in the refrigerator to allow flavors to blend.

ULMACEAE (ELMS)

This family of evergreen or deciduous trees and shrubs consists of about 45 species in 7 genera. Most have mucilaginous substances in leaf and bark tissue and alternate, simple leaves with offset bases and smooth or serrated margins.

AMERICAN ELM, SLIPPERY ELM
Ulmus americana, U. rubra

Native

Edible: samaras, cambium, new growth leaves
American elm was a historically popular shade tree in towns and cities, but many were wiped out by Dutch elm disease that was introduced from Europe in 1941. The disease is still present today, occasionally killing elms before they reach maturity.

Description
Both species are medium to large trees with spreading branches and broad crowns and have alternate, simple leaves that are ovate to obovate with pointed tips. Their leaves are on short petioles, with asymmetrical bases and margins that are doubly serrate. *U.*

americana generally grows larger and fruits earlier, has gray bark with deep grooves and flattened ridges, and its twigs are gray and smooth. Its leaves are up to 5" long, with a smooth, shiny blade surface. *U. rubra* has bark that is dark gray to reddish brown, with shallow grooves and flattened ridges; twigs that are densely hairy when young. Its leaves are up to 8" long with a rough blade surface. Both species have drooping clusters of oval to roundish, winged fruits called samaras. Each fruit is a flattened, single seed surrounded by a papery thin wing up to ½" across, often with a notched tip.

Habitat/Range

U. americana is primarily a bottomland tree, but can be found in upland woodlands, savannas, roadsides, and a wide range of habitats with moist to dry soil conditions. It can tolerate temporary periods of flooding. Range is throughout the eastern United States, west to the Dakotas and Texas. *U. rubra* is found on dry and rocky upland slopes, streambanks, and roadsides, but attains largest size in bottomlands, river terraces, and moist lower slopes. Range is throughout the eastern United States, west to Nebraska and eastern Texas. Absent from upper New England and the southern half of the Gulf States.

Uses

Samaras are tasty raw as a trail nibble or salad addition, best when collected early when the wings are tender and green. New-growth leaves and samaras are also good steamed, in stir-fries, or added to any cooked dish. After the wings dry and turn brown, rub off the papery skin and use the remaining seed in cooked dishes. The mucilaginous cambium is also edible after cooking. It has antioxidant and antimicrobial properties, and is used as a tea to treat sore throats, eye irritation, and acid reflux. To treat sore throat or acid stomach, strip a bit of the inner bark off a small twig, chew for a bit, and swallow the thick sap as it develops. The bark also makes a tough cordage fiber.

Warnings/Comments

The bark's mucilaginous properties can slow absorption rates in the gut, so it's probably best to use it separately from other medications. It can be purchased in raw, powdered, or capsule form and has been commercially available since 1847 as the main ingredient in Thayer's Slippery Elm Throat Lozenges. *U. parviflora* (Chinese elm) and *U. pumila* (Siberian elm) are planted ornamentally and have similar uses.

URTICACEAE (NETTLES)

This family has worldwide distribution and comprises about 2,625 species grouped into 53 genera. Many have stinging hairs on the surfaces of stems and leaves.

WOOD NETTLE, STINGING NETTLE
Laportea canadensis, Urtica dioica

Native

Edible: shoots, tender top leaves, seeds

This delicious, but sometimes unwelcome, plant is easily encountered in the Ozarks. Take a walk bare-legged through weedy vegetation near riparian bottomlands and you'll know when you find it. The leaves and stems are covered in hollow hairs, acting as tiny hypodermic needles that inject a mix of formic acid and other alkaloids into the skin, causing a short-lived itchy rash. Fortunately, a couple of antidote plants are usually nearby. Jewelweed (*Impatiens capensis*) and curly dock leaves crushed and rubbed on the rash will quickly relieve the itch.

Description

Unbranched, hairy stalks are 2'–5' tall. Leaves are on long petioles, spaced alternately on the zigzagged upper third of the stalk. Individual leaves are 3"–7" long, hairy, broadly ovate, with coarsely toothed margins. Seed heads form as small clusters at leaf axils, often forming a larger panicle at the stem apex. Small leaflike appendages hold tiny seeds on the underside.

Wood nettle shoot at collection stage

Wood nettle seeds

Habitat/Range

This perennial likes rich, moist soil, where its rhizomes can spread to form large colonies in wooded stream and river bottoms, shaded, deep hollows, bases of slopes, swamps, and near wooded ponds. Range is throughout eastern and central North America.

Uses

Emerging mid-spring, shoots are great as a cooked vegetable; newer leaves and tender tops of mature plants can be used as a potherb or in soups till the seed clusters appear in late summer–fall. The stinging hairs are softened after a short boil. The dried leaves added to boiling water make a nice tea. Seeds can be used as a grain, collected by drying the tops and shaking over a flat surface. A trick to eating the raw leaves: Pick a tender top leaf and roll it into a tight tube (like a cigarette); keep tightly rolling the length of the tube to crush the glands containing the toxin. I was skeptical at first, but it works! The tough, outer skin on the stalks can be stripped for use as a superior cordage fiber.

Warnings/Comments

To avoid the stinging hairs, collect with gloves or use large leaves of harmless plants to wrap and protect your hands. The introduced, widespread stinging nettle (*Urtica dioica*) is similar, but has pairs of opposite, usually smaller leaves along the stem. Its uses are similar to wood nettle, but it tends to have a stringy texture and isn't as flavorful. Both species have numerous medicinal properties.

Stinging nettle

VIOLACEAE (VIOLETS)

Viola, this family's best-known genus, is herbaceous; most of the 806 species and 25 genera are shrubs or small trees. Many cultivar species are commercially available, sold as violets or pansies.

COMMON BLUE VIOLET
Viola sororia

Native

Edible: flowers, young leaves

Description
A low-growing perennial that emerges from rhizomes as a basal rosette. Leaves are hairy, up to 3" long and across, generally heart shaped, with blunt-serrate (scalloped) margins. They typically grow in bunches up to 4" tall and 6" across. Flowers are borne singly on smooth stems and are usually taller than the leaves. Most species have 2 upright and 2 lateral bearded petals and a lower, nectar-holding small petal that serves as a landing spot for insects. Petal color can be dark blue to nearly white, with a pale lavender center and streaks at the throat.

Habitat/Range
Found mostly in moist soil conditions, open woodlands and borders, rocky slopes, savannas, near ponds and streams, roadside ditches; common in lawns. Range is eastern North America and Canada, west to Texas and the Dakotas.

Uses

Raw flowers and young, tender leaves are a nutritious and beautiful salad addition. Leaves can be steamed, sautéed, used in cooked dishes, and used as a thickener in soups. Flowers can be candied, jellied, added to pancakes and other cakes, used as a garnish, or frozen into ice cubes for drinks. Used medicinally to treat a number of ailments, both internal and external.

Field pansy

Warnings/Comments

Vitamin-rich violets may contain double the amount of vitamin C than citrus per weight, and double the amount of vitamin A than spinach. There are more than 20 species of *Viola* in the Ozarks, some exhibiting very different leaf forms and petal color than the heart-shaped *V. sororia*. All have similar flower structure and are edible. *V. bicolor* (field pansy) is a small plant with orbicular to spatulate leaves, pale purple ¼" flowers, and has a pleasant wintergreen smell and flavor. *V. pedanta* (bird's-foot violet) has 3–5 deeply divided strap-like lobes and large, showy, pale lavender flowers, occasionally with two dark purple upper petals. *V. pubescens* (downy yellow violet) has typical violet leaves, with yellow flowers that arise from leaf stems.

RECIPE

Violet/Redbud Flower Tart

2½ cups redbud or violet jelly

3 cups coconut milk

1 teaspoon dried redbud or violet flowers

3 pods star anise

3 teaspoons agar

½ teaspoon xanthan gum (optional)

1. Mix ingredients cold in a pan; heat slowly until mixture is hot in the middle and sets up on a frozen plate. Skim or strain out solids.

2. Pour into molds and decorate with fresh violet, redbud, or other seasonal flower petals

---

VITACEAE (GRAPES)

This family consists of 910 known species in 14 genera, most of which are tendril-bearing woody vines with fleshy fruits.

RIVERBANK GRAPE (AKA FROST GRAPE)
Vitis riparia

Native

Edible: fruits, leaves

There are eight species of *Vitis* in the Ozarks. Fruits of several species are excellent, but some aren't particularly palatable. My favorite is the large, tough-skinned *V. rotundifolia* (muscadine) found in the southern Ozarks and Missouri Bootheel. I learned about them from Arkansas locals, and had to read about them in a book before I knew the name wasn't spelled "muskydime."

Description

A perennial branching woody vine, often climbing to 65' into the forest canopy. Older vines can become quite large, with dark reddish-brown shredding bark. Younger vines are gray or brown, with slight ridges. Nonwoody climbing young stems are smooth, yellowish green to reddish, with tendrils opposite the leaves. Alternate leaves are generally orbicular, up to 6" long and 5" across, usually palmate with 3 pointed lobes, broadly toothed margins, and a base cleft at the petiole. Blooms May–June; clusters of tiny yellowish-green flowers form opposite new leaves on drooping panicles up to 5" long. In July–September, female flowers mature to drooping clusters of round, bluish-purple fruits, each up to ⅜" across and containing several small, pear-shaped seeds.

Habitat/Range

Found in a number of conditions and habitats, most commonly in river bottom forests, mesic woodlands, bluff bases and ledges, borders of damp prairies and meadows, streambanks, fencerows, and roadsides. Range is mostly the eastern and midwestern United States and Canada. Absent from Alabama to South Carolina and Florida in the east, the southwestern desert states to Idaho in the west.

Muscadine grapes

Uses

Great for a trail nibble; dandy for jams, preserves, and syrups; but chiefly known for making wine. Fruits can also be seeded and dried into raisins or fruit leather. Always look for ground fall around high-reaching vines. Young tender leaves can be added to salads, used as a flavoring for dill pickles, or steamed to make rolled dolmas with fillings of your choice. Terrestrial runners and young vines make great basket material. Larger vines can be used as an emergency pure water source. To collect the watery sap, cut the vine as high as you can reach, then cut at the ground. Hold the cut section upright and drink the sap as it drips out, or collect it into containers. This is less productive in dry seasons. Seeds can be pressed to harvest grapeseed oil.

Warnings/Comments

The fruits of the toxic *Minispermum canadense* (moonseed vine) contain a single, flattened seed with a small notch in the edge (looks like a cookie with a bite taken out). Its leaves are palmately-lobed similar to grape, but without toothed margins, and it doesn't have the forked tendrils as with *Vitis* species. Always check the seeds before consuming. Variation of wild species and hybridization between wild and cultivated varieties can make specific ID problematic for *Vitis* species, but all true grapes will contain the familiar pear-shaped seeds.

Moonseed vine

Moonseed fruits PHOTO BY JOHN OLIVER

MONOCOTS

The monocots are a group of around 80,000 species, and make up about 23 percent of all angiosperms. Its two largest and most diverse families are the orchids and grasses, which make up nearly half of all monocot species. Others include onions, garlic, asparagus, lilies, tulips, daffodils, and palm trees. They are characterized as flowering plants having a single embryonic leaf (cotyledon) in the seed, with leaves that are often narrow and linear with parallel veins running the full length and flowers that are in multiples of three. Its root systems are usually fibrous or rhizomatous; some species form root bulbs.

ALISMATACEAE (ARROWHEADS, WATER PLANTAINS)

This cosmopolitan family comprises between 85 and 95 species in 11 genera. Most occur in temperate regions of the Northern Hemisphere and are found in aquatic habitats such as ponds and marshes. Several have edible rhizomes, leaves, and flower buds.

COMMON ARROWHEAD (AKA WAPATO, DUCK POTATO)
Sagittaria latifolia

Native

Edible: corms, leaves, petioles, flower stalks

Description

A semiaquatic, often colony-forming perennial with arrowhead-shaped basal leaves and 1 or more flowering stalks. Root system consists of fibrous rhizomes, occasionally producing numbers of starchy root corms. Leaves are on erect, stout petioles up to 20" tall, with blades up to 14" long and 10" across, but often smaller and narrower. Blades have conspicuous, generally palmate parallel veins, smooth margins, and reverse-pointing basal lobes similar in length or longer than the primary blade. The smooth, round flower stalk is often the same height or slightly taller than the leaves, with several whorls of 2–3 flowers, 1"–2" apart. Lower pistillate flowers form a bur-like bud that becomes a roundish seed head. Upper staminate flowers are showy, with 3 rounded white petals surrounding a small globe of yellow stamens.

Habitat/Range

Found in shallow water or mud in mucky ditches, sloughs, seeps, marshes, borders of ponds, and along slow-moving streambanks. Range is throughout continental United States and Canada. May be absent from a few western states.

Uses

Corms are edible after peeling; best when boiled, baked, or roasted and used like potatoes. They can be candied, pickled, or sliced thin, dried or roasted, and ground into flour. Young freshly-unfurled leaves, petioles, and early flower stalks can be boiled as vegetables or used in cooked dishes. Flower petals make a nice nibble or salad garnish. The fall seedpods and fresh growth on tips of rhizomes can be eaten raw or cooked. Corms were traditionally harvested by indigenous peoples, who waded barefoot into a partially submerged patch, locating the corms by feel with the feet and then using toes to dislodge so they float to the surface. A garden rake is also useful, as the corms are often at different depths throughout the muck.

Warnings/Comments

Peltandra virginica (arrow arum) has a similar leaf structure, but with a prominent midrib and radiating pinnate veins; its flower structure is a spathe and spadix, typical of arums. It is present in the Ozarks only in wetlands near the Missouri bootheel. Most arums have cell structures that contain calcium oxalate crystals (raphides) that can embed into your mouth and tongue like tiny glass slivers if eaten raw. There are 7 species of *Sagittaria* in the Ozarks. *S. brevirostra* (midwestern arrowhead) and others are similar to *S. latifolia*; a couple related species have linear cattail-like leaves.

COMMELINACEAE (DAYFLOWERS, SPIDERWORTS)

This herbaceous family comprises 41 genera and 731 known species found in both the Old and New Worlds, several of which are grown ornamentally. Their flowers are short-lived, most lasting less than a day.

ASIATIC DAYFLOWER
Commelina communis

Introduced, with similar natives

Edible: leaves, stems, flowers

Description

An herbaceous sprawling annual with vine-like stems up to 3' long. Stems are round and smooth, with slightly swollen nodes that can take root. Alternate leaves are ovate to lanceolate, sessile or clasping at the stem, up to 5" long and 2" wide, with smooth margins and pointed tips. Flowers appear May–October, borne singly on 1"–2" stalks forming at the leaf axil. Each flower is ½"–1" across, with 2 erect bright blue petals and a small pale lower petal. Protruding from the center of the flower are 3 yellow upper staminodes, 2–3 short lower stamens, and a white style. The flower emerges from a curved, folded spathe, developing into a seedpod containing 2 seeds.

Habitat/Range

Found in bottomlands, moist forest borders, roadsides, croplands, lawns, gardens, near dwellings, moist fencerows, and roadsides. Prefers damp, disturbed habitats, but can colonize wherever conditions permit. Native to Asia, found nearly globally due to anthropogenic distribution. Range is the eastern United States and Canada, west to Texas and the Dakotas; also found in Oregon and Washington.

Uses

Young, tender stems and leaves are sweet and slightly mucilaginous; can be chopped and eaten raw in salads, steamed or boiled as a potherb, or added to stir-fries, soups, and other cooked dishes. Used medicinally for thousands of years in China due to its unique compounds and qualities. The plant is grown industrially in Japan to make commelinin, a complex blue pigment derived from the flower petals that was historically preferred by artists.

Warnings/Comments

Five species of *Commelina* occur in the Ozarks. Some are native; all are fairly similar. Occasionally cultivated as an ornamental, it is closely related to the "wandering Jew" houseplant. It can spread quickly to become a garden or agricultural pest.

Ohio spiderwort

OHIO SPIDERWORT (AKA BLUEJACKET)
Tradescantia ohiensis

Native

Edible: shoots, leaves, flowers, seeds

Description
A clump-forming herbaceous perennial with a smooth, zigzag stem up to 3' tall. Alternate, arching blue-green leaves are up to 15" long and 1" across. They are widest at the base and thinner at the tip, with a fold at the midrib, clasping the stem at thick nodes. Blooms May–July, with short-lived flowers appearing a few at a time in umbel-like clusters at the stem apex. Individual flowers are triangle shaped, up to 1½" across. Each flower has 3 rounded petals and 6 bright yellow anthers at the center that are surrounded by a small cluster of fine, deep-blue filaments. Colors can vary to blue, lavender, purple, rose, and occasionally white.

Habitat/Range
Found in open to shady conditions in prairies, glades, old fields, pastures, bluff openings, savannas, openings and borders in open upland forest, and disturbed ground along roadsides and railways. Range is the eastern United States and Ontario, west to Texas and Nebraska.

Uses
Shoots and young stems can be eaten raw in salads, cooked as a vegetable, or used in soups and other cooked dishes. Leaves can be used similarly, but have a mucilaginous quality and can get astringent and less palatable with age. Flowers can be candied or added to salads. Seeds can be roasted and ground for a slightly bitter flour additive. Used medicinally for a number of ailments. The mucilaginous sap is used to treat insect bites and skin conditions. Root is used as a laxative.

Warnings/Comments
Missouri has 8 *Tradescantia* species, including the endemic white-flowered *T. ozarkana* (Ozarks spiderwort), found on rich wooded slopes and ravines. Recent studies discovered that the flower can detect minute amounts of gamma rays more accurately than a mechanical dosimeter. The blue filaments surrounding the stamens turned pink when subjected to amounts of radiation as small as 150 millirems. All *Tradescantia* species can contain needlelike calcium oxalate crystals (raphides) in their internal tissues, and are rarely reported to cause minor skin irritation.

CYPERACEAE (SEDGES)

This large, grasslike family has 5,500 known species described in about 90 genera, with water chestnut and papyrus sedge being two of its better-known species. Stems are characteristically triangular in cross section; leaves are spirally arranged in three ranks.

YELLOW NUTSEDGE (AKA CHUFA NUT, TIGER NUTSEDGE)
Cyperus esculentus

Native

Edible: tubers

Description

A colony-forming, grasslike sedge with long, slender leaves and an erect, central stem up to 2' tall. The rhizomes often form small, elongated tubers, sold commercially as "tiger nuts." Leaf blades are produced in 3s and are connected by sheaths around the lower segment of stem. Each leaf is up to 1½' long and ½" wide, gradually tapering to a sharp point, with a distinct channel on the upper surface midrib. Flowers appear in midsummer or fall as a cluster of yellow floral spikelets in an umbel or compound umbel at the main stem terminus and on the ends of variable-length branches. Flowers mature to tricornered, flattened ovoid seeds.

Habitat/Range

Found in moist or disturbed areas, in gardens, lawns, fields, prairies, ditches, wetlands, borders of ponds, lakes, and streams. Range is throughout the Eastern Hemisphere, most of the continental United States, and Canada. Absent from Wyoming and Montana.

Chufa, or tiger nuts PHOTO BY WREN HAFFNER

Uses

The nutlike, striped tubers have a sweet, slightly hazelnut-almond flavor and can be eaten raw, candied, boiled, roasted, or used as an almond substitute in confections. Tubers can be dried, ground, and used for flour. Add the flour to water, sugar, vanilla, and cinnamon to make a sweet *horchata*-like beverage. Seeds are edible and can be cooked as a cereal or dried and ground into flour.

Warnings/Comments

Due to its aggressively colonizing nature, nutsedge is listed as an agricultural or horticultural pest in some areas. It was widely cultivated as a food crop in ancient Egypt and in most of Europe, and is being rediscovered today as an alternate, healthy food source. Tiger nuts contain a type of starch that is a beneficial prebiotic fiber, helping burn fat and reduce hunger. Recent studies have found that its dietary-resistant starch may improve insulin sensitivity and help reduce elevated blood sugar levels. *Cyperus rotundus* (purple nutsedge) is a similar sedge originally from India, but with purplish flowers and less-flavorful tubers. Some compare its flavor to menthol VapoRub, but it can be improved by soaking in water for several days then drying.

RECIPE

Tiger Nut Horchata

(Adapted from Ian Giesbrecht's recipe at Ozark Mountain Jewel)

1 cup tiger nuts

7–8 cups water

¾–1 teaspoon ground, dried cinnamon or dried spicebush berries

2–3 tablespoons honey

Agave nectar or other sweetener

Small splash of vanilla flavoring

1. Wash and scrub the tiger nuts thoroughly; soak them overnight.

2. Add water to a saucepan with the nuts and other ingredients; bring to a low simmer for 5 minutes while stirring.

3. Place all ingredients in a blender and blend until smooth. Pour the milk mixture into a nut milk bag or several layers of cheesecloth, and squeeze all the milk out.

4. Transfer milk to a large glass container and refrigerate until ready to drink. Serve chilled, topped with nutmeg, allspice, or other similar spice. Serves 3–4

LILIACEAE (LILIES, GARLICS, AGAVES, ASPARAGUS)

This large family has 4,075 known species in 254 genera, including many of agricultural or horticultural importance. Most grow from bulbs, but a few grow from rhizomes. Several species are quite toxic.

WILD ONION
(AKA ONIONGRASS, FIELD ONION, CROW GARLIC)
Allium vineale

Introduced, with similar natives

Edible: all parts
Many non-foragers have become foragers by smell when they first discover wild onion while mowing lawns where it had colonized. This serves as another good reason to keep your lawn untreated and chemical-free—many great food plants and mushrooms can show up there when conditions allow.

Description
A colony-forming herbaceous perennial with a central flowering stem and long, slender tubelike leaves emerging from a papery-sheathed bulb. Leaves are up to 10" long and hollow, first emerging as a small rosette. A round, smooth flowering stem up to 3' emerges from older bulbs, with sparse alternate leaves connected to the main stem by papery sheaths on the lower segment. The flower stem terminates in a teardrop-shaped bud covered in a papery membrane, eventually splitting to expose a flower head of small purplish flowers and/or a clump of aerial bulblets up to 3" across, each with a long green tail. There

PHOTO BY LANDIN HOLLIS / 500PX 500PX PLUS

Wild onion aerial bulblets

Wild onion bulbs

are similar native species. *A. stellatum* (glade onion), found in glades and prairies, has narrow, flat leaves and showy purple flowers. *A. canadense* (wild garlic) has flat leaves and white, pale pink, or purplish flowers. *A. cernuum* (nodding onion) is similar, with nodding flower heads. All members of the genus *Allium* emit a strong onion or garlic odor when crushed. Generally, onions have hollow leaves, and garlics have flat leaves.

Habitat/Range

Found in pastures, lawns, roadsides, woodland borders, croplands, waste areas, and along roadsides. Prefers disturbed habitats. Native to Europe, it has naturalized throughout the eastern and midwestern United States and Canada, west to Oklahoma and Nebraska. Also found in the West Coast states and Montana.

Uses

Tender leaves can be chopped and used as chives. Bulbs can be used as flavoring in raw or cooked dishes, dried and crushed for onion powder, or preserved in brine and pickled, much like any other garlic or onion.

Warnings/Comments

Always smell-test to confirm ID, and be aware of possible toxic look-alikes such as *Nothoscordum bivalve* (false garlic) that have no garlic smell. Wild onion can be an agricultural pest, and it can taint cow's milk when included in their forage.

False garlic

Wild Onion Seasoning Ash

This simple process is an ancient way to preserve the flavor of strong herbs like garlic or onion and can be used in a number of ways.

To make seasoning ash, place bundles of wild onion tops or other flavorful seasoning greens in a shallow pan and bake at 425°F for about 3 minutes. Turn and bake another 3 minutes, until all are a rich brownish black but not yet smoking. **Note:** Thicker plants, like store-bought onions and thick-leaved herbs, will need to be baked longer.

After cooling, pulverize with a *molcajete* or coffee grinder. Use the ash to dust meats and vegetables before roasting, add to soups and cooked dishes, or make a paint or drizzle. These are made by mixing 1–2 teaspoons of ground plant ash with 2 teaspoons walnut oil and ½ teaspoon sea salt. Brush over baked breads, meats, and vegetables, or drizzle over savory cooked dishes.

WILD HYACINTH (AKA EASTERN CAMAS)
Camassia scilloides

Native

Edible: bulbs (see "Warnings/Comments")

Description
This native perennial produces a roundish root bulb up to 1½" across, often forming large colonies. Grasslike, linear leaves emerge as a basal rosette and are smooth with smooth margins, up to 12" long and less than ½" wide, with a prominent midrib, pointed at the tip. Blooms April–May with an erect, smooth central flower stalk up to 2' tall, terminating in a raceme-like cluster of up to 50 flowers; 2–3 bract-like leaves often form below the flowers. Individual flowers are ¾"–1" across, each with a bright green central ovary, yellow anthers, and 6 narrow petals that are pale blue or lavender, rarely white.

Habitat/Range
Found in moist prairies, glades, old fields, rich upland and bottomland forests, moist savannas and open woodlands, bluff ledges, and along streambanks. Occurs throughout the eastern United States, west to Texas and Kansas, north to Ontario, east to Pennsylvania and Georgia. Absent from Florida.

Uses
The starchy bulb can be eaten raw, roasted, boiled, or dried; used in soups or any cooked dish. Has a potato-like taste, but slightly sweeter. They are best when harvested after the tops have wilted.

Warnings/Comments
Care must be taken with ID to separate wild hyacinth from the similar but toxic eastern death camas (*Toxicoscordion nuttalli*), which is present but rare in the Ozarks. The two are easiest to tell apart when in bloom. *T. nuttalli* has white flower petals that are shorter and broader, and are on longer stalks than *Camassia* (see "Poisonous Plants"). Identify when blooming to make sure the entire colony is *Camassia*, as the bulbs without foliage are hard to differentiate. Do not consume unless identification is 100 percent positive! As with all natives, and especially when harvesting roots, harvest sparingly and collect only when encountered in large colonies.

TROUT LILY
(AKA DOGTOOTH VIOLET, ADDER'S TONGUE)
Erythronium albidum

Native

Edible: all parts

Description
Leaves are elliptical, 3"–6" long, either single or in pairs, slightly fleshy and appearing waxy. Only plants with mature, paired leaves will bloom; single-leaved immature plants are infertile. Color is dull green with brown to maroon mottling. *E. mesocherum* has

narrower leaves, usually without mottling, with flower petals not recurvate. Flower is a nodding, single bloom on a single 4"–7" stalk from each set of paired leaves, with 6 recurved tepals and 6 reddish-brown protruding stamens. *E. albidum* and *E. meso-chorium* have white to bluish-white flowers. *E. americanum* and *E. rostratum* have yellow flowers. Large colonies of single leaves may be encountered, maturing in 4–6 years to form the paired leaf that eventually blooms. Root is a deep, often elongated corm, suggestive of a dog's canine tooth—thus the name dogtooth violet (a misnomer, as it is not related to the genus *Viola*).

Trout lily root

Range/Habitat

Found in open woodlands, rich forested slopes, hollows, bottoms, and shaded alluvial soils. Range is the eastern and midwestern United States and Ontario, west to Texas and South Dakota, east to Georgia and New York. Absent from the Carolinas.

Uses

All aboveground parts are sweet and tasty as salad greens while still tender. The single, immature leaves are often found in large colonies and can be harvested without impairing the plant's ability to set seed. The sweet, tender root can be eaten raw or cooked. It is best in spring, when the natural sugars are still present; can get a bit tough and starchy later in the season.

Warnings/Comments

All species are said to be slightly emetic, so consume only small quantities. I've eaten fair-sized amounts in salads with no ill effects, but I wouldn't recommend filling up on them. There are approximately 20 species of *Erythronium* in North America, found mostly in moist, forested habitats and montane meadows. As with all natives, collect sparingly, and never collect roots unless found in abundance.

ORANGE DAY LILY (AKA DITCH LILY)
Hemerocallis fulva

Introduced

Edible: all parts

A big surprise in my early foraging was discovering that the ubiquitous ditch lily that grew in our yard was a very tasty edible. The sautéed buds are one of my seasonal favorites.

Description

This introduced perennial forms fibrous roots with fleshy tubers, and its leaves emerge as a basal rosette. Basal leaves are up to 2' long, linear, with a partially folded midrib and parallel venation, and swordlike pointed tips. They become arched at maturity. One or more stout, erect flower stems emerge from the center of the rosette. The stems are up to 5' tall, round, smooth, and unbranched till near the apex. Podlike 3-segmented buds up to 5" long emerge at the terminal ends of the branched stem, forming blooms in May–August. Flowers are funnel shaped, dull orange, up to 5½" across, with 3 petals and 3 smaller sepals that are backward-curving. Each flower lasts only a day, thus the name.

Habitat/Range

Found in old flower gardens, abandoned homesites, cemeteries, fields, thickets, roadsides, and disturbed streambanks; widely planted as an ornamental. Occurs throughout North America and eastern Canada. Absent from California, Nevada, and the desert Southwest. Native to Eurasia, with global anthropogenic distribution due to cultivation.

Uses

The white portion at the base of innermost young leaves has a sweet flavor when eaten raw. Young leaves and shoots can be added to salads. Young-growth flower stems can be cut into segments and cooked as a vegetable. Unopened flower buds have a slight radish-like bite and are delicious raw, even better as a side dish after a quick sauté in butter. Mature flowers can be added to soups as a thickener, or fried in tempura batter for fritters. Young, soft tubers are excellent when sautéed, boiled, or roasted.

Warnings/Comments

Some report a laxative effect if eaten in large quantity. Reported to cause allergic reaction in some, so consume sparingly the first time. Some true lilies in the genus *Lilium* are toxic. They grow from a root bulb instead of tubers, with leaves occurring up the flower stalk and flowers that last more than a day. To confuse the matter, some *Hemerocallis* species are sometimes erroneously referred to as tiger lily, which is actually a *Lilium* species. More than 60,000 cultivars have been bred from *Hemerocallis*, not all of which are edible.

SOLOMON'S SEAL
Polygonatum biflorum

Native

Edible: shoots, roots

Description

An elegant, herbaceous perennial with a single, slightly zigzagged stem emerging from rhizomes. Stem is unbranched, round and smooth, usually arching, up to 3' or longer. Pale green, alternate leaves are up to 5" long and 2½" wide, sessile, ovate to elliptic, smooth, with prominent parallel veins and smooth margins. Flowers appear May–June, typically occurring in pairs that droop from the stem on short peduncles at leaf axils. Individual flowers are pale green to white, consisting of a narrow, tubular corolla up to ¾" long, with 6 short lobes surrounding the rim. Fertilized flowers produce a blue or purple round berry that is about ½" across.

Habitat/Range

Found in rich bottomland or upland forests, moist rocky slopes, wooded valleys and ravines, shaded seeps, springs, and streambanks. Range is the eastern United States and Canada, west to the Rocky Mountain states. May be absent from Colorado.

Solomon's seal shoot at collection stage

Uses

Young, tender shoots can be eaten raw in salads, cooked as a vegetable, or used in soups and other cooked dishes. Best collected when the leaves are still curled around the stem. Discard leaves if they are bitter; older stems can become fibrous. Rhizomes can be eaten raw, roasted, used in soups and other cooked dishes, or dried and ground for a flour additive.

False Solomon's seal

PHOTO BY ANDREI STANESCU ISTOCK

Warnings/Comments

As with all natives, avoid harvesting unless found in quantity, and always leave plenty for future growth. Two plants are sometimes mistaken for Solomon's seal when first emerging: *Maianthemum racemosum* (false Solomon's seal) has similar stem/leaf structure, with a showy white flower cluster at the stem terminus. *Uvularia* species (bellworts) have branched stems and yellow, long-petaled drooping flowers. Fortunately, both are also edible and can be used similarly to *P. biflorum*.

Large-flowered bellwort

PHOTO BY CYNTHIA SHIRK, STOCKBYTE

MELANTHIACEAE (BUNCHFLOWERS, TRILLIUMS)

This family of herbaceous perennials, previously grouped within Liliaceae, has been recently reclassified. Comprising 173 species in 17 genera, it is found only in the Northern Hemisphere. Its leaves are alternate, whorled, linear, or mostly basal and spirally arranged.

PHOTO BY DEBORAH TYLER

TRILLIUM (AKA WAKE-ROBIN, TOADSHADE)
Trillium sessile

Native

Edible: leaves, flowers

Description
This distinctive perennial has 3 whorled, simple leaves, 3 sepals, and 3 petals atop a smooth stalk, up to 1' tall. Leaves are up to 4" long and 3" wide, oval to ovate, green with lighter mottling, with parallel veins, smooth margins, and blunt tips. Blooms April–June, with green, upright sepals enclosing the petals in a teardrop shape. The sepals eventually open to lie flat on the leaves, exposing purple petals up to 3" tall.

Habitat/Range

Found mostly in rich soil conditions, in moist bottomlands, benches along streams, wooded slopes, and ravines. Range is the eastern United States, west to eastern Kansas and Oklahoma, north to Michigan, east to New York and Georgia. Absent from most Gulf Coast states.

Uses

Trillium is a great salad addition with a unique flavor, and it can be boiled as a potherb with other greens. Trilliums are best collected before the flower opens. A colony will often have many immature leaves without flowers; those can be collected without interfering with reproduction. Do not pull up by the stem; some report that it can affect future reproduction. Pinch off leaves at the top of the stem, or just take a leaf or two from each plant, leaving the flower. If not found in abundance, just admire their beauty and leave them be.

Warnings/Comments

Roots and fruits are reported to be slightly toxic and can cause vomiting if consumed. This plant doesn't do well outside its original habitat, and attempts at transplanting are usually unsuccessful. There are 7 species of *Trillium* in the Ozarks, including the rare *T. pussilum* var. *ozarkanum* (Ozark dwarf wake-robin). It is the only local species with a flower held about the leaves by a stalk.

SMILACACEAE (GREENBRIERS)

The family consists of a single genus with 255 known species and occurs throughout the tropical and warm temperate regions of the world. Most have woody roots and a climbing or vining form. Some have woody vining stems, often with thorns; others are herbaceous and thornless.

GREENBRIER (AKA CATBRIER, BLASPHEME VINE)
Smilax spp.

Native

Edible: shoots, young leaves, roots

Hiking off-trail in the Ozarks can be hazardous. Years ago during songbird research fieldwork, I got tangled and fell while attempting to walk across the top of a 3-foot-high thicket of greenbrier, and it took a while to extricate myself. My skin was so scratched and bloodied that while walking the road out, someone in a car slowed to a stop by me, saw my bloodied neck and shirt, and then sped off! A friend later saw my scratches and asked if I'd been wrestling bobcats. Falling into a greenbrier thicket can definitely evoke some bad language; thus the nickname "blaspheme vine." At least the plant has redeeming values: The young shoots are delicious.

Description

Numerous *Smilax* species are found in the Ozarks. All are stout, woody, green vines, most with thorns or spines. They often form thickets or climb trees and structures up to 25' using the tendrils at the base of leaf stalks. All species have petioled, alternate, simple leaves up to 5" long and 3" wide. Leaf blades are shiny green, heart shaped or lanceolate to oval with smooth margins. *S. glauca* has smaller leaves with white blotches and pale undersides. Leaves of *S. bona-nox* are often wider at the base, narrowing sharply to the tip. Stems of *S. hispida* are covered in dark bristly spines instead of irregular thorns. *S. herbacia* lacks thorns. Most species have small yellow-green flowers that form in umbel-like clusters arising from leaf axils; flowers mature to clusters of ¼" purplish-black berries.

Habitat/Range

Found in a variety of forested and open conditions, thickets, fencerows, dry to mesic forest, glades, bluffs, old fields, and dry edges of bottoms. Range is throughout the southeastern United States.

Uses

Tender tips of shoots, tendrils, and young leaves are great as a trail snack or in salads. They can also be steamed or lightly boiled as a vegetable or added to cooked dishes and soups; some describe the taste as similar to asparagus. Younger roots of most species are edible when boiled or roasted. Larger roots can be dried or roasted and ground for use as a flour.

Historically, the root pulp was mixed with sassafras root, molasses, and a bit of corn and allowed to ferment into the drink sarsaparilla. The berry juice is edible, although most aren't particularly tasty.

Warnings/Comments

Roots and berries contain numerous healthful compounds and phytochemicals and are used medicinally to treat a number of ailments. The low-growing, thornless wild sarsaparilla (*Aralia nudicaulis*) was used to make the beverage of the same name, but it is rarely found in the Ozarks.

TYPHACEAE (CATTAILS)

This marsh-dwelling family consists of 51 species in 2 genera, and is characterized by having two-ranked leaves and a brownish, compact spike of unisexual flowers.

COMMON CATTAIL
Typha latifolia

Native

Edible: all parts
It would take a small book to thoroughly describe all the uses of cattail; it is truly "nature's supermarket"!

Description

Cattail head and peeled stem

A tall, colony-forming wetland perennial with long, narrow leaves and a brown, sausage-like flower spike; 6 or more erect or arching leaves up to 7' long and 1" across emerge from an oval core. A slender, round flower stalk up to 8' tall emerges from the center of the core, developing a terminal, cylindrical flower spike divided into 2 parts. The narrow, upper staminate spike develops pollen and withers away soon after flowering. The lower pistillate spike is up to 1½' long and 1½" across, maturing to the familiar brown seed head we know as a cattail. In late fall, the flower heads explode into seed-bearing white fluff for wind distribution.

Habitat/Range

Associated with open conditions, water-saturated soil/mud, or standing/slow-moving water up to 1½' deep. Forms extensive colonies in marshes, sloughs, edges of ponds and lakes, and wet ditches. Occurs throughout the United States and Canada.

Uses

The white base of inner, emerging leaves is sweet and slightly cucumber flavored; great as a trail nibble. Larger leaf clusters can be peeled of outer leaves to expose the white core, called Cossack asparagus; it can be eaten raw or cooked. The young, green flower head and stalks can be cooked as a vegetable before maturity. The yellow pollen can be harvested from mature flower heads and used as a flour additive or added to soups and other foods as a nutrient and flavor boost. The pointy, lateral shoots emerging from rhizomes are tasty raw or cooked. Harvest while still whitish, before they curve upward to start new growth. Rhizomes can be harvested all winter and processed for the starch. One method is to peel it and pound it in water to produce a thick slurry; allow it to settle before pouring off the water. Add the slurry to soups, breads, etc. The root can also be peeled and cut into thin slices, dried thoroughly, then ground in a food processor or grain mill to produce a starch/fiber mixture. Put the mixture in a jelly bag suspended in a sealed jar; agitate to settle out the powder for use as a flour additive or substitute. Store a bit until late summer when the pollen is available, then combine both with a bit of water. Form into patties and bake for tasty cattail cakes. The long leaves make good thatching for shelter or can be woven into mats, sandals, or hats/visors. Dried stalks make a serviceable hand-drill fire spindle. The fluffy seed head fibers make good fire-starter, or stuff them between layers of clothing for emergency insulation. Soak the dried cattail in animal fat or oil and place it in a hollow stick or length of rivercane to make a torch.

Warnings/Comments

When harvesting rhizomes in winter, look for last year's flower heads to make sure they are cattails, not similar-appearing marsh plants. Leaf stalks should be mild flavored and roundish to oval, not flattened.

APPENDIX A: GETTING STARTED

Learning about plants is much like any endeavor; the more time spent with it, the more useful it becomes. As with mushrooms, it is dangerous to be casual about identification when consuming foraged plants. Many edible plants such as dandelion are so common that they are instantly recognizable. A good practice is to start with easily identifiable species and work up to identifying and using the more unfamiliar ones as you learn. While hiking, carry this and other books in the field as a guide. Spend time studying this and other books and online sources, and then compare that information with what you see in the field before trying new species. One of the best ways to learn is to do as our pre-technological ancestors did, by seeking out and cultivating relationships with teachers and mentors. It is also helpful to plant or visit a garden and familiarize yourself with the edible "weeds" that pop up. Many of our weedy garden invaders were brought by early colonists from Europe and other countries because they were valued for food or medicine. Look for these common plants in disturbed ground, urban waste areas, and un-mowed edges of untreated lawns or farm fields.

The Ozarks region is blessed with many hiking trails in the numerous national and state forests and other public lands, which are always good places to encounter native species. Many state and federal parks and local organizations offer wildflower or edible plant walks and programs. These activities are great for expanding your plant knowledge and meeting other people with similar interests. I learned to familiarize myself with plants by keeping wildflower and other field guides handy in accessible places, such as the coffee table next to the couch, the bed stand, and, of course, in the bathroom.

Tools and Equipment

The only tools needed for collecting are gloves, collection bags or baskets, and a small lock-blade or fixed-blade knife. A stout walking stick is always handy when navigating the steep hills and hollers; if needed, you can turn it into a digging stick by fire-hardening the smaller pointed end. You can use your phone's camera to get pictures for later comparison with other sources. Plant identification phone apps can be helpful as learning tools, but they are an unreliable source when collecting for consumption.

A few processing tools are good to have on hand. For grinding nuts and seeds, use a *molcajete*, *mano* and *metate*, or mortar and pestle. For softer roots and shoots, use a food mill. To harvest the pulp from soft fruits, use a cone-shaped colander (chinois) or a wire strainer. For processing roots for flour and nuts for milk, use milk nut bags or cheesecloth. If you are cooking where there is electricity, a blender, food processor, and coffee grinder can make short work of some of the processing.

Preparing Your Harvest

Many plants described here can be used for stand-alone side dishes or combined with other ingredients for a main meal. Some plants may have strong or unique flavors that are unpalatable by themselves but can add zest to dishes with milder ingredients. Keep in mind that our flavor preferences have been conditioned by generations of selective breeding that has produced watery, sweet food crops, while foraged foods may contain strong and unfamiliar flavors. It's always fun to experiment and discover new and amazing combinations!

Salads

The basic salad served in many restaurants contains iceberg or leaf lettuce with a few chopped tomatoes, onions, and shredded carrots. A fancy salad or salad bar may have up to three or four types of greens, with an additional eight or so added vegetables, nuts, and fruits. A wild-foraged spring salad may have twenty or more species of greens and flowers in a mix of mild and strong flavors, providing a different taste combination in every bite! Many of my students have commented that after tasting these salads, they find it difficult to go back to plain ol' lettuce. Early fruits like wild strawberries, blueberries, and serviceberries are

good additions, as are any available wild nuts and seeds. Toasted insects such as crickets or larvae are nice for a nutty-flavored salad topping, just as you would add sunflower seeds (see appendix C: "Edible Insects"). Several plant species that are considered "spring greens" die back in the heat of summer then put on new growth with the cool and damp late-fall weather. While out hiking, carry a small bottle of balsamic or seasoned rice wine vinegar and a bit of seasoned salt. It takes very little time to throw together a great salad, using a flat rock, a slab of dead wood, or a plastic collection bag for a bowl. Euell be glad you did!

Potherbs

Potherbs are greens that need to be cooked to improve texture, flavor, or edibility. The leaves of plants such as wintercress and curly dock may have excessively bitter or tart flavors that are reduced by cooking. Wood nettle has stinging hairs that are rendered harmless by cooking, and pokeweed greens contain toxins that need to be cooked off by one or more boilings. Many salad greens or shoots that are eaten raw can also be cooked as potherbs and vegetables. I grew up eating greens or wilted salads dressed with hot bacon grease and white vinegar, but there are many alternatives, such as lemon juice and seasoned rice wine, balsamic, and fruit vinegars. Make your own wild vinegar with leftover skins and flesh remnants still attached to seeds after processing fruits such as pawpaw, persimmon, passionflower fruits, autumn olive berries, wild grapes, wild plums, and other large-seeded fruits used for jelly or syrup. Wild fruit syrups added to unflavored vinegars can produce very nice flavor combinations.

Seeds and Nuts

Nuts such as hickory, walnut, and hazelnut can be dried in the shell after hulling and stored for several months. They are fine raw, but roasting often improves the flavor and lengthens shelf life during dry or frozen storage. The nuts can also be shelled and pickled in brine, but they will need to be thoroughly rinsed before use to remove some of the salt. Many smaller seeds can be sprouted, or dried and stored in jars then roasted and ground for a flour additive. See "Tools and Equipment" for grinding and processing tips.

Fruits and Berries

Most fruits are best when eaten fresh, but many can be dried or processed into jellies, preserves, syrups, or sauces.

Syrups are made by simmering fruits in a bit of water then straining to remove larger seeds if present. Jellies usually require additional pectin, but some fruits contain it naturally. Make unsweetened fruit syrup to use as a sauce for meats and other foods. The syrup can be sweetened later and used as a dessert topping or in beverages.

Make your own wild vinegar with fruits past their prime and leftover skins and flesh remnants still attached to seeds. Use fruits such as pawpaw, persimmon, autumn olive berries, wild grapes, wild plums, passionflower, and other large-seeded fruits used for jelly or syrup. To make wild fruit vinegar, use these proportions (scale them up for larger batches): ⅓ cup sugar to 4 cups fruit or fruit scraps; water to cover. If fermentation doesn't start after 3 days, add champagne yeast. Fruit flies carry bacteria that can aid the process, so leave the container uncovered for a bit to let them have access. They can be strained out later. Other ingredients can be added, such as spruce buds, juniper berries, herbs, and anything else that will produce interesting flavors.

Wild fruit syrups added to flavored or unflavored vinegars can produce very nice flavor combinations. Use fruit syrups and cider or other fruit vinegars to make a fruit "shrub" drink. These "drinking vinegars" were often combined with wines or spirits. They were quite popular in ancient Rome and colonial America as a way to kill bacteria in the water while preserving perishable summer fruit. There's no set recipe. Just add a bit of vinegar to plain or sparkling water, sweeten with fruit syrup or your favorite sweetener, then add muddled or chopped fruit or berries. For preservation, the mix should have about 5 percent acidity, resembling lemonade in tartness.

Fire cider is great in fruit shrub drinks for a boost to the immune system, and there are many recipes available. Here's my favorite:

RECIPE

Fire Cider

Fill a lidded gallon jar half full with equal amounts of:

grated roots of horseradish, ginger, and turmeric

½ bulb garlic, chopped

½ onion, chopped

1 lemon, sliced

1–2 habanero or other hot peppers

Small handful of peppercorns

Optional: savory or medicinal wild herbs, fruits, and other seasonal plants

Fill the rest of the jar with apple cider or wild fruit vinegar and let sit for 4–6 weeks. After the initial strong flavors mellow, enjoy sipping the cider straight. Or mix with fruit juice or water in a shrub drink. It also serves as a wonderful and unique salad dressing vinegar.

APPENDIX B: PLANTS BY FOOD TYPE

Salad Greens and Flowers (spring–early summer)

Aniseroot, 29
Asiatic dayflower, 186
Basswood, 120
Broad-leaved plantain, 138
Canadian honewort, 26
Chicory, 45
Climbing false buckwheat, 140
Common blue violet, 178
Common cattail, 210
Common chickweed, 80
Common mallow, 119
Corn salad, 78
Cut-leaved coneflower, 43
Cut-leaved toothwort, 66
Dandelion, 51
Eastern redbud, 96
Field sorrel, 144
Garlic mustard, 61
Greenbrier, 208
Henbit/Deadnettle/Ground ivy, 109
Lamb's quarter, 20
Orange day lily, 201
Oxeye daisy, 42
Perilla and other mints, 115
Purslane, 150
Shepherd's purse, 65
Smartweeds, 142
Solomon's seal, 202
Spicebush (leaves), 7
Spreading chervil, 25
Spring beauty, 149
Tall wild lettuce, 47
Trillium, 206
Trout lily, 199
Violet/Yellow wood sorrel, 130
Virginia waterleaf, 57
Wild onion, 194
Watercress, 70

Potherbs/Vegetables (late spring, summer, fall)

American lotus, 124
Chicory, 45
Common amaranth, 17
Common burdock, 34
Common evening primrose (shoots), 128
Common milkweed (shoots, seedpods), 31
Curly dock (shoots, leaves), 146
Cut-leaved coneflower, 43
Eastern prickly pear, 72
Lamb's quarter (shoots), 20
Oxeye daisy, 42
Pokeweed, 136
Sow thistle, 50
Tall thistle (peeled shoots raw or cooked, leaves cooked), 38
Tall wild lettuce, 47
Water lily, 126
Wintercress, 63
Yellow pond lily, 126

Fruit/Berries (late spring–early fall)

Autumn olive, 85
Blackberry/Black raspberry/Dewberry, 162
Blackhaw, 15
Common elderberry, 13
Common hackberry, 75
Downy hawthorn, 155
Downy serviceberry, 153
Ground cherry, 169

Ground plum, 94
Mayapple, 55
Missouri gooseberry, 102
Pawpaw, 2
Persimmon, 82
Prickly pear, 72
Purple passionflower, 133

Red mulberry, 122
Wild black cherry, 160
Wild blueberries, 87
Wild grape, 181
Wild plum, 158
Wild strawberry, 157

Seeds/Beans (summer–fall)

Amaranth, 17
American/Slippery elm samaras
 (spring), 173
Broad-leaved plantain, 138
Climbing false buckwheat, 140
Common evening primrose, 128
Common mallow, 119
Curly dock, 146

Hog peanut/Trailing fuzzy bean, 89
Lamb's quarter, 20
Lotus/Yellow pond lily/Water lily, 124–26
Maple samaras (spring), 164
Purple passionflower, 133
Purslane, 150
Tall thistle, 38
Wood nettle, 175

Nuts (late summer–fall)

Acorns, 99
Basswood, 120
Black walnut, 107
Buckeye, 164

Butternut, 107
Hazelnut, 53
Hickory, 104

Roots/Tubers (some spring or winter only)

American groundnut, 92
American lotus, 124
Aniseroot, 29
Common evening primrose, 128
Greenbrier, 208
Hog peanut, 89
Orange day lily, 201
Solomon's seal, 202

Spring beauty, 149
Trout lily, 199
Water lily, 126
Wild carrot, 27
Wild ginger, 5
Wild hyacinth, 197
Yellow nutsedge, 191
Yellow pond lily, 126

Seasonings

Aniseroot, 29
Evening primrose (root), 128
Garlic mustard, 61
Horseweed, 33
Mints, 111
Peppergrass, 69
Sassafras, 9

Spicebush, 7
Sumac, 22
White smartweed, 142
Wild carrot, 27
Wild ginger, 5
Wild onion, 194
Wintercress, 63

Beverages

Aniseroot, 29
Blackberry/Black raspberry/
    Strawberry, 157, 162
Dandelion/Chicory root, 45, 51
Hackberry, 75
Mints, 109
Purple passionflower, 133

Sassafras root, 9
Strawberry/Blackberry leaf (tea), 157, 162
Sumac berries, 22
Tiger nuts, 191
Wild ginger root, 5
Wood nettle, 175

APPENDIX C: EDIBLE INSECTS

If you're out to collect food plants, it's a good idea to snag any edible insects encountered on your foray—toasted, those insects will add extra protein and fat calories to your meal. They contain as much or more protein per weight than meat, and insect larvae contain good fat calories. Studies report that 20 percent of the world's population consume insects in 80 percent of existing countries, leading many to believe that this is a new frontier in sustainable food production.

Always cook insects and larvae by toasting or boiling or by adding them to other cooked dishes. Generally, most bugs have a nutty flavor when toasted, and toasted larvae are absolutely delicious as a snack or salad topping. Common foraged insects include adult crickets, grasshoppers, cicadas, dragonflies, mayflies, and spiders and the larvae of wasps, ants, beetles, and acorn weevils. If your garden is ravaged by tomato hornworms or Japanese beetles, collect them to incorporate into your meals. I encountered a couple of surprises when diving into entomophagy: The chemical that creates the "stink" of green stink bugs turns to pure delicious flavor when toasted, and the flavor of cooked wolf and orb weaver spiders is similar to buttery beef. (Who knew?)

Process most insects by removing legs and wings, as adult insect legs can have tiny hooks, and the wings burn easily. Spiders are cooked whole. Be bold and give it a try! Insects to avoid are centipedes, millipedes, fuzzy caterpillars, and some of the larger adult beetles.

APPENDIX D: INDUSTRIAL FOOD VS. WILD FOOD

The plants we buy in the supermarket might look and taste great, but humans have apparently been selecting away from the medicine in our plant foods for more than 10,000 years. (Again, who knew?) When we transitioned from our hunter-gatherer past to an agrarian lifestyle, we selected a few plant varieties that were larger, sweeter, easier to grow, and easier to process than their wild counterparts. This resulted in our consumption of a much smaller variety of plants than had been relied on earlier, especially bitter herbs, tough roots, and plants that required a high level of processing. Studies show that many of these undomesticated plants contain high levels of anthocyanins, polyphenols, and other phytonutrients that are essential to good health. Modern commercially-grown food contains more sugar and water and fewer vitamins, minerals, and nutrients in comparison.

Recent archaeological studies of cultures in the areas of transition confirm that early Neolithic herder/farmers lost bone density, developed cavities, were more susceptible to disease, and even grew physically shorter when compared to those still employing a hunter-gatherer lifestyle. A stable but less diverse food supply was apparently less beneficial to health than an intermittent but extremely varied food base. The combination of large-scale livestock meat production and mechanized agriculture that allowed for higher yields worked together to reverse some of those early negative health trends, but may have created new ones in the process.

Much of our current agricultural system is primarily concentrated on cultivating monocrops for their ease of mass production, uniformity, marketability, and long shelf life. However, many aspects of modern food production can deteriorate nutritional quality in many ways. Croplands can become exhausted of natural minerals and nutrients, requiring heavy use of fossil fuel–derived fertilizers and pesticides/herbicides. Factor in the long harvest-to-table time in shipped foods, loss of species variety due to monocropping, the lack of genetic diversity in individual plants, the reliance on grain-based and high-sugar foods, and yet-unknown possible long-term health and environmental impacts from high-tech genetic tampering. Taken together, these developments have produced a food source that is not as beneficial to health as it could be, and may be contributing to common health problems such as diabetes and obesity.

In areas without available foraging opportunities or an abundance of wildlands, there are still great alternatives to industrial food. These include small-farm agritourism, urban farmers' markets, and farm-to-table dining opportunities that offer organic, heirloom plant varieties and wider selections than can be found in most supermarkets.

GLOSSARY

Reproductive Structure

Achene—A small, dry one-seeded fruit that does not open to release the seed.

Anther—Pollen-containing part of a stamen.

Beak—A prominent pointed terminal projection of a seed or fruit.

Bract—A modified, usually small, leaflike structure often positioned beneath a flower or inflorescence, differing in shape or color from other leaves.

Calyx—A collective term for the sepals of one flower; the outer whorl of a flower, usually green.

Catkin—A flowering spike of trees or shrubs, typically downy, pendulous, composed of flowers of a single sex, and often wind pollinated.

Corolla—Collective term for the petals of a flower.

Cotyledon—The embryonic leaf or leaves in a seed, the first part to appear in a germinated seed.

Cyme—A flower cluster with a central stem bearing a single terminal flower that develops first, the other flowers in the cluster developing as terminal buds of lateral stems.

Dioecious—Male and female reproductive organs occur in separate individuals.

Disk Floret—Any of a number of small tubular and usually fertile florets that form the central disk. They are often accompanied by ray florets and are commonly found in the family Asteraceae. In rayless flowers, the flower head is composed entirely of disk florets.

Drupe—A fleshy fruit with thin skin and a central stone containing the seed.

Inflorescence—The complete flower head of a plant, including stems, stalks, bracts, and flowers.

Keel—The bottom two fused petals of a flower, shaped like a boat keel; characteristic in some legumes.

Lenticels—Raised pores in a woody stem that allow gas exchange between the atmosphere and the plant's internal tissues.

Ovary—The enlarged basal portion of the pistil in the female organ of a flower; usually matures to a fruit.

Panicle—A loose branching cluster of flowers.

Pappus, or pappus bristles—A tuft of hairs on a fruit or seed.

Petaloid—Resembling the petal of a flower.

Pedicel—A stem that attaches a single flower to the inflorescence, arising from a peduncle.

Peduncle—Main stalk of an inflorescence.

Pistil—The female organs of a flower, comprising the stigma, style, and ovary.

Raceme—A flower cluster with the separate flowers attached by short equal stalks at equal distances along a central stem.

Rays, or Ray Florets—Radiating petals surrounding a disc floret, as in Asteraceae.

Sepal—Individual parts of a flower's calyx that enclose the petals. Typically, green and leaflike.

Spike—An unbranched, indeterminate inflorescence in which the flowers are without stalks.

Stamen—The male organ of a flower, usually consisting of a stalk called the filament and a pollen-bearing anther.

Staminode—A flower with stamens but no pistil.

Stigma—The sticky stem of the pistil of the female reproductive system.

Style—A long, slender stalk that connects the stigma and ovary.

Tepal—One of the outer parts of a flower (collectively, the perianth). The term is used when these parts cannot easily be classified as either sepals or petals.

Umbel—An inflorescence in which a number of flower stalks or pedicels, nearly equal in length, spread from a common center.

Umbellet—A secondary umbel in a compound umbel, such as the carrot.

Leaf Descriptions

Apex—Tip or uppermost part.

Axil—Upper angle between the stem and a leaf.

Basal rosette—Leaves forming a circle at the base of the stem and growing to a similar length, somewhat resembling the petals of a rose.

Bipinnate—Doubly pinnate; a compound leaf with individual leaflets that are pinnately divided.

Blade—Flattened part of a leaf.

Cauline—Leaves growing on the stem, usually the upper parts.

Compound—A leaf with several leaflets; it usually detaches from the main stem at a node.

Crenate—Scalloped, or having blunt or rounded teeth.

Crisped—Finely curled, as with the edges of leaves and petals.

Dentate—Toothed or serrated.

Deltoid—Triangular; shaped like the Greek letter delta.

Elliptic—Oval, with a short or no point at the tip.

Entire—Leaf with smooth edges around the entire margin.

Lanceolate—Long and wider in the middle; shaped like a lance tip.

Margin—Edge of a leaf blade.

Node—Part of a stem where leaves or branches arise.

Orbicular—Round, circular.

Oblanceolate—Much longer than wide and with the widest portion near the tip.

Obovate—Teardrop-shaped; stem attaches to the tapering end.

Ovate—Egg-shaped or oval; with a tapering point and the widest portion near the petiole.

Ovate-acute—Ovate with a sharp tip.

Palmate—A compound leaf that is divided into leaflets whose stems emanate from a single central point.

Palmately lobed—A leaf that is divided into three or more distinct lobes, like the palm of a hand with outstretched fingers.

Peltate—A roundish leaf with the petiole connected at the center.

Petiole—A leaf stalk.

Pinnately compound—Having two rows of leaflets on opposite sides of the axil.

Pinnatifid—Pinnately lobed.

Rachis—Main stem of a pinnate leaf.

Reniform—Kidney shaped.

Serrate—Toothed, with asymmetrical teeth pointing forward; saw-toothed.

Sessile—Leaf attached directly to a stalk with no stem or petiole.

Sinus—A notch or depression between two lobes or teeth on a leaf.

Spatulate—Spoon shaped; having a broad flat end that tapers to the base.

Ternately compound—A compound leaf with leaflets arranged in multiples of three.

General Terms

Adventive—Introduced but not fully naturalized.

Angiosperm—A plant that produces flowers; seeds are enclosed within a hollow ovary. This group represents around 80 percent of all plants, including herbaceous plants, shrubs, grasses, and most trees.

Annual—Plant that completes its life cycle in one year.

Biennial—A plant that completes its life cycle within two years. It usually forms a basal rosette of leaves the first year, producing flowers and fruits the second year.

Corm—A fleshy, round stem base or tuber-like root used as a storage organ; usually covered with leafy scales.

Cosmopolitan—Worldwide distribution in appropriate habitats.

Mesic—A habitat with a moderate amount of moisture.

Perennial—Plants that go dormant over winter and regrow more than two years.

Rhizome (Rhizomatous)—A perennial underground root or stem, usually growing horizontally.

Stolon—A slender, prostrate or trailing stem (runner) that produces roots and occasionally erect shoots at its nodes.

INDEX

ABOUT THE AUTHOR

Bo Brown has taught outdoor skills for nearly thirty years. His initial interest in plants was bolstered by decades of work as a songbird biologist and field technician, where habitat vegetation studies required accurate plant identification. One of these studies led to a nine-year position as a naturalist for the Missouri Department of Conservation.

Bo currently conducts programs in Stone Age wilderness survival skills, foraging, and nature education through First Earth Wilderness School, originally founded in 1992 with Don Brink. Classes are held at Bo's property on the Niangua River, surrounded by 8,000 acres of state forest. He also presents programs for regional public and private schools, museums, and nature centers, including weekly primitive skills demonstrations and foraging walks throughout the summer at Dogwood Canyon Nature Park, a Johnny Morris property in southwest Missouri near the Arkansas border. He instructs at several large national primitive skills gatherings and has been cohosting the Bois D'Arc Primitive Skills Camp & Knap-In with Don Brink since its founding in 1998. He is also a professional musician, performing locally and nationally in several area bands. He bases these various activities from his log home on wooded acreage near Springfield, Missouri.

Information on his foraging programs and other activities can be found at firstearth.org or at the Facebook page "First Earth Wilderness School."